ABOUT THE COVER:

The lovely ladies on the cover are my sisters. My actual blood sisters. In the photo I may look like a stereotypical "ladies man" because I got beautiful women around me, but how does the image change when you realize they are my sisters? I wrote this book to help men change harmful perspectives about how we see women. We should treat everyone like they are our sisters and our brothers.

WHAT PEOPLE ARE SAYING ABOUT LADY'S MAN:

One of the final exercises of the ritual of passage of boyhood into manhood is when the newly initiated novice is able to speak to those behind him of the lessons he has learned. LADY'S MAN is a penetrating, personal and poignant message in the language and the images of this day and time by Dr. Obari Cartman that represents a successful completion of his transition through the stages of boyhood and initiation into manhood. As Malcolm X internalized the messages of manhood taught by his Man Teachers: Marcus Garvey, Elijah Muhammad, Dr. W.E.B. DuBois-- who transmitted the messages of their teachers, Frederick Douglas, David Walker, Bishop Henry McNeil Turner and Dr. Edward Blyden—in the language and context of this day and time, Dr. Cartman now has demonstrated his successful matriculation into African Manhood with the message and lessons he has penned in LADY'S MAN. He imparts the accumulated wisdom of those who have facilitated his passage into manhood by his articulate translation of the messages of our African Griots and Ancestors, by his ability to speak in the language and the images of this generation and those who apply this timely guide by the lessons he has learned that they may soon demonstrate their successful passage by translating and transmitting to those behind them the eternal truths encapsulated in the appropriate imagery and language of their time and place. The Elder teachers have taught Dr. Cartman well and their integrity has been maintained through his ability to clearly and honestly speak the words of old in the language of this time that those who must follow in his steps may preserve the liberating and instructive wisdom of their message. Congratulations, Dr.Obari Cartman, for a successful transition, transformation with impeccable clarity and honesty enhanced by your personal journey.

-Na'im Akbar, Ph.D.,

Student of the African Mind

In this deeply compelling and manifestly brilliant book, Dr. Obari Cartman taps into the rich legacy of the greatest African griots of time past, in order to weave a series of 21st century life-affirming stories of hope, salvation, and love. His primary audience is the teeming masses of racialized and silenced young Black men of America, desperately seeking to rediscover the sacred and civic path that leads to voice, identity, and power. Using language that is very accessible, he delivers masterfully in all areas. Not since James Baldwin's *The Fire Next Time* has there been a book that speaks so powerfully to the souls of young Black men. The book is a must read for all, and to the extent that it successfully answers the stubborn and elusive American question of "how did we get here?" it may very well be the most important book a young Black boy or man will read in his lifetime.

-Dr. Stanley Howard

Founder and President of The Law and Civics Reading and Writing Institute (A Chicago-based education think tank), and author of *Righting America's Wrongs: A Best Practices Manual for Educating Black Male Youth.*

Lady's Man is brutally honest and provides concrete suggestions for improving black female and male relations and extended family development that is so critical to the African community in America. I would encourage everyone in our community to read this creative, thoughtful, reflective, and insightful exposé by Dr. Cartman.

-Dr. Conrad Worrill

Director and Professor of the Carruthers Center for Inner City Studies (Northeastern Illinois University)

This book had my attention from the first to the last word. And had me do alot of self reflecting as a man. This is a MUST READ, for women too, but, especially for the black man of present day.

-Courvosier **"Hunid Proof"** Randolph

young Black man

Dr. Cartman is one of the wise and visionary writers of his generation. Don't miss this book that can change your life!

-Dr. Cornel West

Dr. Cartman's instant classic is a must read for anyone that knows and loves a black man. As a mother with the incredible task of helping a boy become a man in these daunting times I am encouraged to know there are thoughtful, compassionate and courageous men like Dr. Cartman that are sharing their wisdom, challenges and triumphs that will help provide guidance for all of our sons.

-jessica Care moore

Poet, Publisher, Activist, Moore Black Press

Dr. Cartman has done a brilliant job in empowering Black males to reach their full potential and respect females. Obari clearly understands the nation is only as strong as the family.

-Dr. Jawanza Kunjufu

author of Countering the Conspiracy to Destroy Black Boys

Dr. Obari Cartman presents an overview of the Afrocentric journey that contributes to the creation of today's young Black men. Dr. Cartman then provides: 1) a guide to self-discovery for these young men; and 2) the tools needed to "sculpt" their future selves and to find their purpose. As an urban school educator who experienced great success in teaching our young, this book would be a powerful teaching and learning tool.

-Dr. Carmen L. C. Palmer

EdVK Founding President

Educational Village Keepers, Inc

LADY'S MAN

LADY'S MAN
CONVERSATIONS FOR YOUNG BLACK MEN
ABOUT RELATIONSHIPS AND MANHOOD

Dr. Obari Cartman

www.DrObariCartman.com

Cover design and book layout and design by Cassiopeia: soldesignsinc@gmail.com
Cover photography by Dominique Shepherd: domdigitalmedia@gmail.com
Printed by BCP Digital Printing: www.bcpdigital.com

ISBN 978-0-692-38910-2

DEDICATION

I owe this book to all the young men who were brave enough to share their struggles with me. They thought I was helping them, sometimes. But it was really them helping me, all the time. Those conversations are the true inspiration for my work.

ACKNOWLEDGEMENTS

Modupué Olodumare for being. Modupué Sango and Obaluayé for guidance, protection, humility and power. Modupué Egun.

I knew very early that I could not write this book alone. The first thing I established was a council of elder men to advise me as soon as I had an outline. The years of marriage and parenting combined between my babas Fluke Fluker, Kamm Howard, Carl Hampton, Wekesa Madzimoyo, and Stan Howard provided my ideas with the wisdom necessary for a project of this magnitude and depth. Then having my younger brothers reading drafts like Ben Ford and Courvorsier Jones gave me the intergenerational perspectives I needed.

Malikah Waajid was the first person to give me the confidence to write a book. Her intellect, love, and feedback made this what it is. Lynnette Johnson is another brilliant writer and thinker I'm fortunate to be able to call friend and supporter. And Essence . I would send the 3 of them chapters as soon as I was done, and get almost immediate feedback. Having that type of brilliance so close has been invaluable.

It's really been the incredible women in my life guiding the ideas in the book, providing the most consistent feedback. It's a rather poetic reflection of the work Black women do, often without credit, to contribute to the well-being of Black men. Sona Smith (bff) gets the award for the sweetest encouragement. Thabisile Griffin's feedback was so smart it could be a book on its own. Afrika Porter knows everybody and everything, one can't do anything worthwhile without an Afrika Porter on the team. Melissa Moore was a wonderful editor. But truly, everyone who touched this book while it was in the womb is a powerhouse. Evin Marie, Kimberly M. Harmon, Amara Enyia, Ayo Carter, Brandeis Nilaja Green, Ayesha Jaco, Jennifer Ligaya, Elizabeth Whittaker, Nikala Asante, Rachel Rai Henry, Jikol Lockhart, Kelley Moseley, Africa Brown, Mashaune Hardy, mama Samella Abdullah and Gwen Mitchell of Third World Press. Every one of them contributed something that changed the book. There's a piece of brilliance from each of them in here. And I am forever grateful to them for that.

In the final stretch of this, after realizing writing the book is just the first part and now I have to print the thing and tell somebody about it, I've had a dream team of folk helping me realize my dream. Patrick Oliver, my publishing consultant, told me everything I needed to know to remain independent, efficient and professional. Cassiopeia is a team all by herself. She helped design the cover, she designed the flyers, helped me pass out flyers all over the country, and most importantly she spent hours learning how to design the interior layout of the book so she could do it herself. So many things happened because my talented friends believed in me enough to volunteer their services and accept my modest donations. Many thanks Bryant Cross for the website, Dominique Shepherd for the cover photography,

Dane Verrtah of Hepicat for the Afro Futuristic glyphs, Ben Ford and Paa Kofi for beats that I won't use till the next volume of the mixtape. And I'm ever so grateful to all the magnificent national and international artists that donated their music to the mixtape.

Finally, I must thank my family. For their specific support of this project and their general support of my life. (Although I consider most names mentioned already to be family) I'm grateful for my spiritual family, Baba Ason and the Ajunaku's for helping me connect to the power of our traditions. My extended family from the Institute of Positive Education and the cultural communities of Chicago and Atlanta. My African dance and drum family. My academic family from Georgia State and Hampton University. My Association of Black Psychologists family.

Im grateful for the Jaco family, who I'm fortunate to be forever connected to through my son and the greatest thing that ever happened to me Naseer Hanif. And my blood family: The Holmes, Elms, and the Cartman clan! I can't say enough about how beautiful my family is. Especially my siblings, Teasy, Komo, T-ra, Yin, Jam, Nana, and Char-bear. I wouldn't have chose anybody else to share this journey with.

And to you, reading this now. Whoever you are, however you got this book. I believe it was a part a design greater than all of us, and I'm grateful that our paths have crossed.

Asante sana.

LADY'S MAN MIXTAPE

To Download, Go To:

www.DrObariCartman.com

1. **Artist:** PHENOM, **Song:** Summons, **Album:** Dat Boy Said
2. **Artist:** B.O.B, **Song:** New Black, **Album:** New Black Mixtape
3. **Artist:** Dometi (fka Proph), **Song:** Ex Slave Circa 1836, **Album:** The Malcolm X Mixtape
4. **Artist:** Add-2, **Song:** Modern Day Coons, **Album:** Save Our Souls
5. **Artist:** K-Love, **Song:** SGA
6. **Artist:** Wteve Baker, **Song:** Spiritual Warfare
7. **Artist:** Skipp Coon, **Song:** bravo tengo delta, **Album:** Miles Garvey
8. **Artist:** Phenom ft. Gemstones, **Song:** Put the Guns Down
9. **Artist:** Real T@lk, Song: Jealousy, **Album:** The Talented Tenth
10. **Artist:** Kemet, Song: Super Glue, **Album:**

LADY'S MAN
MIXTAPE: VOL. 1

Curated by:
Dr. Obari Cartman
Mixed by:
DJ Joe Kollege

11. **Artist:** Sa-Roc ft. David Banner, **Song:** The Who, **Album:** Nebuchadnezzar
12. **Artist:** Stic.Man of Dead Prez, **Song:** Champion, **Album:** The Workout
13. **Artist:** Mama SOL & Tha N.U.T.S., **Song:** Manhood, **Album:** Inside Out
14. **Artist:** Hurt Everybody ft. Mick Jenkins, **Song:** Treat me Caucasian, **Album:** Hurt Everybody EP
15. **Artist:** Jasiri X, **Song:** Open Heart Surgery, **Album:** Ascension
16. **Artist:** Dee-1 ft.Alexis Jones and Ambush, **Song:** Accountability Partner, **Album:** Psalms of David II
17. **Artist:** Allah's Apprentice, **Song:** Meditation, **Album:** Appreciation
18. **Artist:** Amir Sulaiman ft. Drea D'Nur, **Song:** Come to the Hills, **Album:** The Opening

TABLE OF CONTENTS

INTRODUCTION

For parents, mentors, coaches, barbers, ministers, and other caring adults

They say Black boys don't read. I disagree. I say too few books are written with Black boys as the audience. I say too many families and schools aren't cultivating the inherent genius of Black boys and encouraging them to read. I say the world is afraid to find out what happens when Black boys turn into powerful Black men.

This book is about family. It's more of a personal book than an expert book. I hope it raises more questions than provides answers. It's designed to facilitate meaningful conversations that result in stronger families. This book focuses on Black families, because that's where I come from. And since it's a personal book, I want to share from a place that I'm most familiar. I hope, though, that people of all races, ethnicities, sexual orientations, classes, religions, and shoe sizes find the book useful. Some topics require specific attention but that doesn't have to cause division.

Black families have lots of challenges, so there are lots of opportunities for solutions. One solution is to develop stronger men. Which will create stronger partners in relationships. And stronger fathers. But first, we must figure out what a "strong man" is. How does one become such a thing, and what are the obstacles? We, as men, have to think and talk about how our relationships with women impact our manhood (and are impacted by our manhood). We must also realize that there's really no such thing as "a strong man". There are many different ways to express manhood. Strength does not always roar. Often strength is compassion. Or tenderness, or humility.

Lots of and organizations programs have been designed to help Black boys. Meanwhile, the most fundamental unit of organization continues to suffer: the family. It is much easier to blame all Black family problems on "the system" but we must also consider how conflict within our own communities is also a factor. We may be hurting ourselves faster than any organizations or programs can help save us.

Most family institutions are structured around the stability of the primary unit: the relationship between adult male and adult female. Black families often include extended members in useful ways. In addition, there are other types of relationships that families are centered around: men loving men, women loving women, polygamous families, etc. This book, however, will focus on one-on-one heterosexual relationships, since that is still the primary arrangement for most Black families. Other family structures must also be written about and discussed, but by someone with more personal experience in those areas than I have. The identity, socialization and power dynamics of same sex and polygamous families deserve specific attention.

We know from the heterosexual divorce statistics, single parent mother statistics and from our own lives that Black folk are having a difficult time creating and maintaining healthy relationships. Often because some of the fundamental elements of successful relationships are missing: trust, compatibility, honest communication, and community support.

There are a lot of books about relationships, but their audience tends to be women. Women are talking in salons, re-posting blogs, going to seminars, having book clubs, watching Oprah's network, and whatever other stereotypical things men think women do. The point is women are encouraging each other to think about healthy relationships more frequently than men. There is no such parallel process for men. So I often wonder, when women figure out all the secrets to the dating game, who are they supposed to partner with?

This book focuses on the men. We should prepare young men for relationships while they're in their early stages of developing identity, manhood, and their ideas about women.

This book is a socialization tool. Too often young men develop their ideas about relationships and women through socialization tools that lack wisdom. A lot of socialization happens through peers, and is guided by media images and messages. Or mis-guided, because media producers are also motivated by money, not just wellness.

The power to change the circumstances of Black families is within us. We have everything we need. Which does not ignore the aggressive, systematic, and diverse attacks against Black families. Embedded in the social, political, and historical narrative of this country and many other countries are deliberate strategies to maintain institutions that elevate White/European descendants and keep Black /African descendants struggling to survive. It's an old story. It's a familiar story. And it's a story that's coming to its end.

As the world evolves so do the challenges of Black people. It's not as simple as a Black vs. White problem anymore. In many cases the sources of attack have become more difficult to detect. As Black people have fought for and achieved access to money, opportunity, and decision making roles we have often had to make compromises to maintain that "success". The ascension of a few has done little to affect the well-being of the masses.

The young men that really need to read this book may not do so willingly. As their parents, mentors, teachers, etc. it will be important for you to create incentives for them to read. For example, don't buy him another pair of shoes or another video game until he has read. Or offer him his favorite meal and some extra time with you after he writes a page of reflection for each chapter. Sit and listen to the music in the mixtape with him and discuss how the themes compare to what he already listens to. Also, since we know too many schools aren't preparing them properly, some young men may have a difficult time actually reading and comprehending, so read it with them. Be prepared to disagree with some of the points I make. That's a good thing, because it creates opportunities to engage young people in critical conversations.

This is a book about relationships. On one hand, it's about fostering healthy relationships between young men and young women. And young men and themselves. At the same time, it is about your relationship, as a caring adult, with the young people in your life. It's not enough to hand the book to a young man. Even if you feel unqualified to guide a young person for whatever reason, this book is designed to assist you. You have to read it with him, talk about where you agree and disagree, stay engaged in conversations and relationships with him, and do your absolute best to show him peaceful, loving, productive relationships by demonstrating it in your own life.

SOMETHING TO KEEP IN MIND. . .

I wrote this book in the same way that I talk, so all the grammar won't be correct. I want it to read like a conversation. This style is good when you're writing in a personal journal. But you shouldn't use this same writing style for an official paper in school. You should never put words like "gotta" in a school assignment. U gotta know when 2 say "have to". For correct grammar and sentence structure you should read different types of books. And it's not about using good English or bad English. There is nothing wrong with the way you speak. As long as you are getting your ideas out clearly. But while in school, and for business, it is important to learn to switch over to what they call "proper English", which educator Dr. Asa Hilliard calls "money English".

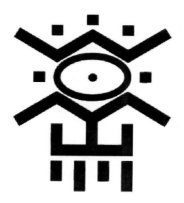

CHAPTER I

WHY IS THIS CONVERSATION IMPORTANT?

Y ou are more powerful than you think. When young Black men decide to use their intelligence and talents to impact the world in positive ways then everything will be different. Until then, the world will stay broken because we keep doing the same things. Changing will be hard, there are lots of people who like things just the way they are. Those people are happy when young Black men only see themselves as athletes, rappers, or entertainers. Or see themselves as superior to women and treat them like toys. Or see themselves as criminals, or pimps, or stupid, or lazy, or worthless. This book will change that.

The World We Live In

The world is run by a small percentage of people. One hundred percent (100%) of the people means **everyone**—every man, woman and child on the planet. So fifty percent (50%) means half the people on Earth. Here's the problem: 5% of the people control the money and resources for the rest of the 95% of people. (Resources = food, water, land, books...all the important stuff.) Seems unfair doesn't it? That a few people have so much power over the rest of us? That's like letting one person on your block be in charge of going to the grocery store to get food for everyone. They can pick whatever food they like. They will keep most of it for themselves. They'll probably give out the best food to their own family. And the rest of the neighbors get whatever food is left, if there is any left. Some people are always left hungry. The world is like that.

Rich people make all the decisions about how cities are organized, how money flows, what gets taught in school, and who gets food and health. Most of the really rich people aren't famous like entertainers or athletes so you don't even know their names. Right now most of those people are White men, especially in the US. Which usually means other White men benefit from the decisions that they make. When people get to be that powerful they try really hard to **stay** that powerful. To keep you from your power they designed a system that has you at the bottom with other so-called minorities, poor people, and people of color, fighting each other for leftovers.

For that system to work, they have to try to convince you that you aren't capable and don't deserve better. <u>And _you_ have to believe them</u>. The attack happens in school, with jobs, with healthcare, using the police and prison, using television and radio…just about anything you can think of. Unemployment and hunger leads to incarceration. Liquor stores are on every corner. Healthy food is on no corner. The laws are unfair. Evictions and foreclosure. Diabetes and high blood pressure. Schools with old wrong books and overworked teachers. Garbage on the streets. Garbage on the radio. Drugs and guns imported from outside the community. Police and judges acting like they're God. Art is taken out of the school, and the list goes on…The attack has to be everywhere because you are **that** powerful.

This book is about the attack on relationships between you and Black women. The people in charge of the world know that if they keep Black men from being strong <u>partners</u> with Black women then you will be easier to control. Especially if most Black children are raised by just one person alone. The people in charge are mostly White, but that doesn't always mean they are the enemy. It's not that simple anymore. Maybe it never was. Slavery in North America never would have been as successful without some Black people who also thought they benefited from it. You're not just a victim. You have power and responsibility. This isn't about hating White people. Most of them don't even realize they're part of a system that puts them on the top and you on the bottom. It's worse than that—most White people were just born into a world where they were already on top so **they don't even think about** how it affects you.

> *"Not every white person is a racist, but the genius of racism is that you don't have to participate to enjoy the spoils. If you're white, you can be completely oblivious, passively accepting the status quo, and reap the rewards."*
—Mychal Denzel Smith [1]

Before we go further, let's be clear about what "White" people means. White is very broad (and so is "Black", but we'll talk about that later). Calling people by their race, like White or Black or Hispanic or Asian, is fairly new in human history, because the idea of RACE is fairly new. We used to define people by smaller sized groups: tribes, villages, ethnic groups. For example, we use the label "White" in the United States to group a bunch of smaller tribes together (Italian, Russian, Polish, etc.) who each have their own separate language and culture.[2] Using 'race' is a lazy way to describe people. White people use it to gain power in numbers. By combining all their smaller groups into one White race they create a majority in the United States, making you a 'minority' (which is far from true in the world).

Individual White people are not the problem. I want this to be clear because I'm gonna say some ugly stuff about some things White people have done (and are still doing) to us, and I don't want you to get pissed off, go back to school or work and punch all the White people in the face. That won't help nobody. It's good to have diverse friends and good relationships with all kinds of people. Just be careful. Don't let anybody trick you into thinking that their stuff is better: their hair, their skin color, their values, their food, their music, their religion, their economic system, etc. And White people are really good at that.

What's wrong?

So what exactly is the problem? What do I mean when I say Black people are losing?

Remember: It'll be important that you ask questions while you read, about everything. Don't take the things anyone says as automatic truth just because they have a Dr. in front of their name or because it's on TV or because it's written in a book.

Here's part of the problem:
- White Americans have 22 times more wealth than Blacks. [3]
- Black males ages 15–19 die from homicide at 46 times the rate of White males their age.[4]
- Death rates from cardiovascular disease, cancer and diabetes are much higher for Blacks than other racial groups. [5]
- Black men and women represent the highest rates of never married. [6]
- African-Americans are twice as likely as Whites to be unemployed. [7]
- There are more Black men incarcerated in the United States than the total prison populations of India, Argentina, Canada, Israel, Lebanon, Finland, Germany, France, and England combined. [8]
- The average 17-year-old Black student has the reading and math scores of the average 14-year-old White student. [9]

Some people will read statistics like these and say *"Well that just confirms what we already thought. Black people are just less intelligent than everybody else..."* OR *"Something is clearly wrong with these people because they have the same opportunities as everyone else blah blah blah"*... Whoever says that is an idiot. They're missing the big picture:

White America has more <u>advantages</u> and Black America has more <u>obstacles</u>. Whites had a 300-year head start in this country. Any country with hundreds of years of free labor would be rich. Then America kinda freed us but started lynching us instead. Then America changed its mind and let us vote and go to its schools and get jobs only if we dressed, talked and thought just like White people. Now America doesn't need Black people for labor anymore. Machines do all the work, so with fewer jobs and without proper education a lot of Black people commit crimes that get us back in prison again, in chains again, working for free again.

The whole time White people have owned almost everything. The land (*wait....how can you even own land?*), the people (*how can you own people??*), the businesses, the government, the schools, the jobs, the radio and television stations...everything. And they just keep passing it down to their children. So they have a head start every generation. And there are times when Black people come together to own and operate their own things, like in 1921 on Black Wall Street in Tulsa, Oklahoma. But then White people just bombed it!

So when you read negative statistics about how "bad" Black people are doing, read them very carefully. We definitely have struggles, but <u>there are also lots of Black folk that are doing</u>

<u>very well</u>:   raising powerful families, inventing new technology, growing food on farms, traveling the globe, writing books, creating schools, solving world problems, etc. Those stories just aren't the ones you see on the news. And when you really think about all the trauma Black people have been through in this country, it's really amazing that we still love each other and contribute as much as we do to the world.

If this is a book for men, what does it have to do with 'ladies'?

The title of this book is **Lady's Man**. You knew that. But you may not know why. I've been called a "ladies man" once or twice during my youth (last year), and as I grow more mature I try hard to change that reputation by changing my thoughts and behavior towards women.   So I called this book **Lady's Man** to flip the whole idea upside down. The apostrophe sign (') at the end of a word changes the meaning of it. That ' sign shows possession, tells us when one thing belongs to another thing. So if I say Dr. Cartman's sandwich, that ' sign tells you that the sandwich belongs to me. It is my sandwich.

This book is called Lady's Man because I belong to the women in my life. I am my mother's son. I am my sisters' brother. I am my niece's uncle. I am here on this earth to serve them and protect them and care for them. I am partly responsible for their well-being.

I think the same is true for all men and all women. Women are the mothers of all of us. There is no breathing man on this earth that did not come through a woman. Yet, we often treat women like they belong to us. Like they are our toys, our objects of pleasure. We use them until we've gotten what we want from them. And that is never, ever okay.

What's wrong with how we treat women?

There are lots of men that treat women with respect and admiration. They do stuff like:
- open their doors
- give up their seats when a woman is standing
- honor their intelligence
- help them carry heavy things or situations
- tell other guys 'it's not cool' when they hear them being disrespectful
- be completely honest with them
- don't curse in front of older women
- speak to women with kindness and not with anger or aggression
- would never raise their voice or ever let any one else think of raising his hand towards women
- organize people in their community to boycott the radio and television stations that play songs and images that make women look like prostitutes
- see women past their gender, as human beings

But then there's other men that treat women with disrespect. They do things like:
- call women bitches or ho's
- support music, images, and language that promote a rape culture
- make fun of women they don't find attractive
- only give attention to women who wear tight or sexy clothes

- pressure women into being more physical than they feel comfortable being
- use their strength to threaten or intimidate
- tell women they like them or are attracted to them just as a trick to get something

You know who you are. You know what you do. At the end of the day, when you're alone in the dark, or early in the morning, brushing your teeth in the mirror—when you look yourself in the eye, only you know the truth. <u>Only you know what you say and do to the women in your life</u>. And you know you're doing the right thing when you can be completely honest and still be proud, for treating women like you would want someone to treat your daughter, mother, sister, or grandmother. You're doing even better when you can teach another man to do the same.

Because no matter what you do, some man, somewhere, is responsible for these numbers:
- Black females experienced intimate partner violence at a rate 35% higher than that of White females, and about 22 times the rate of women of other races. [10]
- Approximately 40% of Black women report coercive contact of a sexual nature by age 18. [11]
- For every African-American/Black woman that reports her rape, at least 15 African American/Black women do not report theirs. [12]
- According to the U.S. Justice Department, nearly one of every five Black women – 19 percent – are raped each year. [13]
- African-American women experience significantly more domestic violence than White women in the age group of 20–24. [14]

There are some monsters amongst us, attacking women in broad daylight. They are attacking your sisters and cousins and will continue to attack your daughters if we don't stop them. I don't know who these men are. Maybe it's you reading this book right now. Maybe you are one of those guys on the news taking advantage of younger women, or using your strength to overpower women, or slipping drugs into their drink and taking advantage of them. If you have done, that a part of me wants to wish something really bad happens to you. But instead I pray that you stop, get the help you need, and work to repair the damage you've done, like your eternal life depends on it.

If you're not one of those monster men, then you probably know him. It could be your uncle, or brother, or best friend. You've heard him say some really creepy and disrespectful things. You may have ignored them 'cause you didn't know what to say. Or maybe you laughed because you felt uncomfortable. But you didn't stop him. Which does not mean it's your fault if another man harms a woman, but it does mean that we are all in this together. When one of us suffers—man, woman or child—all of us suffer.

How will this book help ME today?

You ever hear those stories about billionaires who commit suicide and wonder why they did it? You ever think about how much drugs celebrities do and how much drama they have in their lives? A lot of celebrities seem really sad. How is it that some people get exactly what they want in life, fame and fortune, and still end up feeling miserable?

Sometimes men use women like an addiction. Like an addition to drugs, or alcohol, or power, or shopping, or violence. Some men surround themselves with women to distract themselves from their sadness. Sad isn't a feeling men admit to very often. But there are lots of reasons for men to be sad: unemployment, addiction, children problems, relationship drama, family struggles, poverty, poor health...the list goes on and on. Human stuff. Men struggle with human stuff. And instead of crying about it, or writing about it, or going to church to release it, or talking honestly with our friends about it, we use whatever we can to pretend like everything is okay. When we feel weak we try to mask the pain by looking powerful. And what are the two symbols of power that Black men can have? MONEY & WOMEN.

Let's pause here for a second, before I go on and you keep reading this like, "He ain't talking about me." Let me be more specific about what I mean by sad. Have you ever woke up in the morning and felt so heavy that it was hard to move? Have you ever gotten so frustrated because you felt like everything you did was a failure, so you just gave up? Have you ever gotten so upset that you lost control of your own words or body? Do you expect to go to prison at some point? How long do you expect to live? Do you ever imagine yourself as an 85-year-old man? When was the last time you sat in a quiet room? No mp3 player, no internet, no TV, not eating or drinking, no radio, phone off.... just silent. If you can't do that, it's not because you're bored. It's because those silent moments are when sadness shows up. But only if you haven't dealt with it. If you have dealt with it then those silent moments are when feelings of overwhelming peace show up. And I'm gonna show you how to get that kind of peace, if you haven't figured it out already.

This book is as much about treating <u>yourself</u> better as it is about treating women better. **Black men need to take better care of ourselves**. So we can do a better job of taking care of our families. We were all born with a purpose and too many of us don't know what it is. Too many of us waste our time following somebody else's plan for us. You should wake up every morning asking yourself: *"What is my purpose? Why was I born?"* It might take years to figure out the answer, but once you do then you should wake up every morning asking yourself: *"Am I living that purpose? Am I at least on the right path?"*

One of the easiest ways to know someone has no idea of their purpose is when they say their purpose is to "make a lot of money". That's not a purpose, that's a goal. A purpose is deeper than that, and usually has something to do with making people's lives better. And your purpose almost always has something to do with a natural passion, gift, or talent you have. This is important because *if you don't find your own purpose*, then I promise someone else is waiting to **use you** to live theirs. They will use you to fight their wars. They will use you to build machines and buildings. They will use your intelligence and skills to create cities and nations. They will make money off of you. Then, when they are done with you, they **will throw you away** like an old paper towel. And you will live and die never knowing what true happiness feels like.

So that's why I'm writing this book. Because the time has come for Black people to come together to improve the conditions of our families and our communities. And you're reading this book because **you are now a part of the movement** towards a new world. Where children are fed, where elders are honored, where physical and mental health is a priority, where people are truly happy. And you, Black man, with the blood of the oldest people on the planet running through your veins, have a special task in creating this new world. While everyone else thinks you're in a crisis, while everyone else thinks you have been defeated, I know that you have just been waiting for the perfect moment to awaken that excellence resting deep inside of you. And that moment begins right now.

CHAPTER 2

HOW DID WE GET HERE?

We should always know how we got where we are. Sometimes "where we are" is a place, like going to a new store or visiting someone's house. It's important to pay attention to the directions while we're getting there, so we don't get lost. Sometimes "where we are" is a stage in life. Being lost in a new neighborhood or in life can be very frustrating. Whatever our age—15, 25 or 65—we should be able to think back on our life and figure out how we got there. Retrace your steps: Where were you born and raised? Who was around? How did they treat you? What did they teach you? What were some of the best moments that define you? What were some of the worst?

You have a personal history and should try to understand it if you want to move forward in life. Black people, as a group, also have a history. And we need to know that too if we're going to have a real conversation about what it means to be a Black man and improve Black families.

So here we are, in Black America. More than seven million (7,133,594 to be exact) children (almost 70%) not being raised with a mother AND father in the home.[1] Forty two million black people in the United States, 920 million in the world. These days most of our U.S. tribe prefers to be called African American. Which I agree sounds better than Negroes or Coloreds. We've been in this land they named America for almost 400 years, most of that time in captivity. We know a lot about the USA part of African American: McDonald's, Yahoo, Hip-Hop, Disney, Columbus discovered it on accident and killed most of the people living here, and the rockets red glare the bombs bursting in air. We don't know as much about the African part of **African** American. Which is strange because we've been African for so much longer.

How did we get to America?

Most of the Black people in the Americas and the Caribbean were brought here to work for free for hundreds of years by European terrorists. That's how the United States got to be so rich. Some African people came to "America" long before slavery. Many of them were scientists and explorers who figured out how to travel the world while Europeans still thought the Earth was flat. There's a book about it called ***They Came Before Columbus: The African Presence in Ancient America, by Ivan Van Sertima***. Yes, that means Africans were building ships and studying the stars thousands of years ago. There's a lot you won't learn in most schools about early Africans, how genius we were, and how much we contributed to the world. Because if you knew how powerful your ancestors were, then you'd know how powerful you are.

What happened in Africa before slavery?

Africa has the oldest and richest history on the planet. To begin with, Africa gave the world all its people! (see documentary called "The Real Eve" by the Discovery Channel) Every people on the planet, White, Black, Latino, Asian... everybody, can trace their ancestors back to early Africans. Africans were on the Earth hundreds of years before anyone else. So we built the first cities, were the first doctors, created the first schools, were the first to write, and do math and science, and religion and music.

If you don't believe me there's tons of books that can tell you all about it:

The World and Africa, by W.E.B. DuBois. ***The African Origin of Civilization***, by Cheikh Anta Diop. ***Stolen Legacy: The Egyptian Origins of Western Philosophy***, by George G.M. James. ***African Origins of the Major "Western Religions"***, by Yosef Ben-Jochannan. ***How Europe Underdeveloped Africa***, by Walter Rodney. ***The Destruction of Black Civilization***, by

Chancellor Williams. *Journey to Africa*, by Hoyt Fuller. *Introduction to African civilizations*, by John G. Jackson… just to get started.

One of the ways our early African ancestors were able to build and achieve so much was because of the powerful role <u>family</u> played in their societies. There were different types of families across Africa. Most were headed by one man married to one woman, raising children with the help of a community. Marriage also didn't mean the exact same thing — a lot of the ideas we have now of "romantic love" based relationships came from other cultures over time. In some places in Africa, families with one man married to two or more wives were also common. Those marriages were sometimes more difficult for the men; they had to earn the right to care for several wives. But having more women and children <u>working together</u> in the house also has many benefits.

Marriage in Africa wasn't just about two people liking each other a lot. Parents and grandparents were involved in choosing mates. If a man wanted to marry a woman he usually had to give her family money first, or a symbol of his hard work and ability to provide. Families often lived near or in the same house with other relatives. Whatever the arrangement, it was always true that <u>both the men and the women</u> had extremely important roles for the most important function of family: raising healthy and productive children.

If human history begins with Black people living in Africa with our own nations, governments, military, universities, cities, businesses, churches, etc., then how did White people come and enslave us?

Just imagine: you live in a city today, lets say Chicago, and a couple of your friends wanted to go to St. Louis to turn people there into your slaves (no offense to St. Louis, it's a lovely city). The people there are minding their business—going to school, working, buying houses, raising children. But you want to force them to walk back to Chicago and work for FREE all day. You couldn't just say "Hey St. Louis people I own you all now! Come back to Chicago with me. Oh and your children will also belong to me, too, forever!" Just think about it…. What would it take to make that happen? And how much damage would you do if you broke all the families apart? If you took husbands away from wives and children away from their parents? Brothers and sisters never seeing each other again… When you figure that out, then you'll begin to understand what happened to African people at the beginning of America.

You actually might have a hard time thinking about what you would do to these nice people in St. Louis to make them your slaves. It takes a special kind of sick mind to think like that. Today, we might call those kind of people terrorists, psychopaths, or serial killers (except during slavery, the Europeans didn't want Africans to die—we were only worth money alive). So let me help you think like a European terrorist for a moment…

Instead of thinking about turning another human into a slave, think about training a dog to serve you and obey your commands. The first thing you may notice is that it's harder to train an adult dog. It's much easier to train a puppy. You make the puppy depend on you for food. You physically punish it if it disobeys you. You control its ability to make babies by cutting off its balls. Or if you want more puppies, you force it to have sex. If it barks too loud you put a muzzle on it. If it tries to run away you chain it, or lock it in a cage. White people treated us like animals.

So Europeans came to Africa and stole us?

When we think of this part of the story we often imagine White people sneaking into Africa in the middle of the night to kidnap helpless Africans. That can't be what happened. We were too strong and too powerful for that. And 20 million people (at least) is too many to just kidnap. Africans had more people, knew the land better, had better technology and had more military advantages than our European neighbors. If that wasn't true, Europeans would have just gone to Africa and enslaved us there.

Then what happened?

That is a very difficult and important question. The answer is even more difficult... *It was our fault.*

Using the word 'fault' does not mean our European attackers were not also to blame. But it's not healthy (or true) to depict our African ancestors as only victims of a powerful European oppressor. Yes, they were our enemy. But they were not more powerful, or smarter, or more advanced than us. The White Europeans that came and put your ancestors on those torture ships **must be held responsible for what they did to us.** The countries involved in the trading of people owe us for what they did. That payment should come in the form of land, money, free education, and debt relief for student loans...to begin with.

However, they never could have brought that many people out of Africa without help from some of us Africans ourselves. Saying it was our fault is the difference between saying they sold us into slavery and we sold ourselves into slavery. We lacked then the same thing we lack now: a unifying Black/African identity to connect us wherever we are on the planet. That type of unity would have protected us.

We were divided by tribes and ethnic groups. Some of the groups were at war with each other. We look back at history and wonder how we sold our brothers and sisters into slavery, but we didn't see each other like that. Back then we thought we were selling our enemies into slavery, even if they looked just like us. That's how we were able to trade human beings for things like silk cloth, alcohol, or guns. Plus, at the time, we had no way of knowing how greedy and ruthless those Europeans were.

All humans are born with a natural need to belong. This need makes us form groups. It also makes us have to figure out who's NOT in our group. So we create 'others'. Outsiders. Even enemies. We can become really passionate about claiming our group: our block (east side!), our neighborhood (Brooklyn!), our religion (non-Christians are going to hell!), our country, our sports team, our fraternity/sorority, etc. This same process at its worst will allow a man to kill his brother if he's not a vice lord, GD, BD, blood, or a crip. It's the same thing that allowed a Jewish Holocaust to happen. Or a genocide in Rwanda to happen.

If we want to make sure those kinds of human disasters never happen again, we must figure out a way to belong to separate groups and at the same time see ourselves as belonging to the same African family. So then we will be able to show the world how to belong to one human family.

What exactly happened to us during captivity?

The enslavement of Africans in the Americas was the worst period of suffering and human tragedy from one group to another, ever. A crime against humanity. There are other times when people were enslaved, but it was uniquely brutal in the U.S. That's why I call those Europeans "terrorists". I won't call them "slave owners". We weren't slaves. We were human beings who had been captured. Europeans never 'owned' us. I certainly ain't gonna call them "masters". They systematically created a world full of terror for African people for hundreds of years. So I call them **terrorists**.

At least 20,000,000 (million) people were captured in Africa, by the English, Portuguese, Spanish, French and Dutch.[2] About half of the Africans were tortured to death on the way to America. Some were forced to walk in chains for hundreds of miles from their homes to the ocean. Then they were held in dungeons along the coast of Africa until forced onto ships that carried them across the Atlantic. They lay on the wooden floors of those ships for months, chained together, with barely enough space to move. If they had to pee, shit, or vomit, it happened right where they lay. When women had their period, they bled right where they lay. The women also had extra trauma from being raped more often than men by the European terrorists.

A lot of Africans got sick and died on the ships. Others tried to jump off, but were severely beaten if they got caught. Others refused to eat, but the terrorists forced food down their throats, breaking teeth if they had to. Others fought back and tried to take over the ships. But if Africans got caught, the European terrorists would punish them horribly to discourage the other Africans from even trying to fight. For example, [true story] when the captain of one ship caught Africans fighting back, he responded by "... *making them first eat the Heart and Liver of one of them killed. The Woman [who helped in the revolt] he hoisted up by the Thumbs, whipp'd, and slashed her with Knives, before the other Slaves, till she died.*"[3]

Only 4% of us Africans were brought to USA. The rest were taken to countries in South America, like Brazil. Or to islands in the Caribbean, like Haiti, Jamaica, Cuba, or the Bahamas.[4] That's why the Africans in those countries are truly our cousins, even when they speak different languages. We were just dropped off in different places. Even if we came from the same village or family in Africa.

Once we made it off the ships, we finally got some fresh air, but that also meant the beginning of intense forced labor. Most of the work was in the sugar, cotton and tobacco fields, producing crops to be sold for millions and millions of dollars over hundreds of years. <u>Africans were doing all the work, while White terrorists were taking all the money.</u> Africans also built homes and buildings, were cooks and servants, raised the terrorists' children, made roads, tools and furniture, and any other work there was. Africans were forced to work so long and so hard that many of them were **worked to death**. Skeletons of enslaved Africans were recently found in New York, buried under Wall Street. Studies of their bones showed broken necks and muscles torn apart, because they were worked so hard.[5]

Slavery was a big deal. Twelve US presidents personally held enslaved Africans captive.[6] People went to markets to buy Black people, like you could go to the store to buy a bike today. <u>Christian preachers</u> were in on it. They used quotes from the Bible like 1 Peter 2:18, *"Slaves, submit yourselves to your masters with all respect, not only to those who are good and considerate, but also to those who are harsh."* Or Ephesians 6:5–6, *"Slaves, obey your earthly masters with respect and fear, and with sincerity of heart, just as you would obey Christ. Obey them not only to win their favor when their eye is on you, but like slaves of Christ, doing the will of God from your heart."*

Terrorist preachers forced Africans to practice their version of Christianity, trying to convince us to wait until heaven for freedom. The <u>doctors</u> were involved. A doctor in Louisiana made up a disease called Drapetomania for any African that showed the desire to run away.[7] The <u>politicians</u> were involved. It was against the law to teach enslaved Africans how to read and write.

Africans lived under constant fear and violence. And we're still talking about some of the strongest people on the planet. So the terrorists had to torture them all the time. When it wasn't enough, if an African refused to work, if he or she chose to suffer the torture instead, the terrorists would find a loved one, a child or parent, and torture them until they changed their mind. When you look around and see so many shades of skin color in black people, many of the light-skinned black people today are a result of the white terrorists raping African women. Then their children were born enslaved.

The system of slavery only worked for so long because of <u>constant violent force:</u> rape, beatings, torture, lynchings, murder, and the threat of violence against loved ones.

Did African people fight back?

Absolutely! Always! Black people resisted slavery <u>the entire time</u>. We fought in Africa when Europeans came to take us. We fought on the ships that brought us here. We fought during the years of torture in Brazil and Jamaica and South Carolina when the Europeans tried to break our minds and spirits. We fought for our often short but entire lives while being forced to work.

Sometimes the fighting meant **taking over the ships**, or jumping off of them into the ocean. Sometimes the fighting was **escaping**. We **burned down houses**. We **poisoned** the terrorists' food. We made quilts and songs with secret codes in them to help each other run away. We escaped into the forests and formed hundreds of independent societies. We **made alliances** with Native Americans. We learned our oppressors' language well enough to tell others about the horrors of slavery through newspapers, books and lectures. We prayed to our own gods at night and practiced sacred rituals from our homeland. AND we did a lot of actual fighting—training, making or stealing weapons, and organizing groups of men and women to revolt, battle and kill our attackers.

There's a great book with a lot of those resistance stories called *There is a River: The Black Struggle for Freedom in America*, by Vincent Harding. Or to learn about some of our bravest warriors for freedom, look up: Nat Turner, Harriet Tubman, Zumbi dos Palmares, Nanny of the Maroons, Gabriel Prosser, Toussaint Louverture, Denmark Vesey, The Stono Rebellion, John Brown (white guy), Cinqué of the *Amistad*... just to get started.

Were Africans Able to Have Relationships and Families During Captivity?

"Marsa ["master"] used to sometimes pick our wives fo' us. If he didn't have on his place enough women for the men, he would wait on de side of de road till a big wagon loaded with slaves

come by. Den Marsa would stop the ole nigger-trader and buy you a woman. Wasn't no use tryin' to pick one, cause Marsa wasn't gonna pay but that much for her. All he wanted was a young healthy one who looked like she could have children...." [8]
Those are actual words from an enslaved African about how little power we had to create families.

This is a real advertisement (like a commercial) in a newspaper from New Orleans: *"A Negro woman, 24 years of age, and her two children, one eight and the other three years old. Said Negroes will be sold separately or together as desired."* [9]
They didn't have any problem selling these children apart from their mother.

Henry Bibb was an African who escaped to Canada in 1844 through the Underground Railroad. He wrote back to his terrorist saying, "to be compelled to stand by and see you whip and slash my wife without mercy, when I could afford her no protection, not even by offering myself to suffer the lash in her place, was more than I felt it to be the duty of a slave husband to endure..." [10] Men were powerless to protect their families.

SIDENOTE: If Henry Bibb, during slavery, can learn to write that well, then Black students alive today should never make any excuses about reading or writing not being important enough.

Enslaved Black families had less power in the U.S. than in other places. In countries like Brazil in South America, Black families were protected by the church and some laws that allowed

Africans to marry freely. And married couples couldn't be sold apart. None of that was true in the U.S. "In the United States, the slave husband was not the head of the household; the white owner was the head." [11]

But as bad as U.S. slavery was, it didn't destroy Black relationships. For most of the years between 1880 and 1970 Black people were married at higher rates than White people. Only recently, in the last few decades, have Black people stopped getting married as much.[12] Which means we have to figure out what happened in the past few decades.

Did White Americans stop attacking Black families after slavery was over?

You hear people say "Lincoln freed the slaves." Let's talk about the word freedom for a moment. **A person cannot give freedom to another.** One can only make it more difficult for another to get it. Not being enslaved anymore does not equal freedom. Even today, a person can be 'freed' from prison but still can't vote or find a job. The most minimum thing a people need in order to call themselves free is the ability to control their own food, housing and education. Black people still don't have that.

As long as the mind is enslaved, the body can never be free. Psychological freedom, a firm sense of self-esteem, is the most powerful weapon against the long night of physical slavery. No Lincolnian Emancipation Proclamation or Johnsonian Civil Rights Bill can totally bring this kind of freedom.
—Martin Luther King, Jr.

We talked about slavery in detail because it was such a major attack against Black people, but during the 100 something years since slavery, a lot has been done in the United States to make it difficult for us to build and maintain healthy families. None of it stopped us completely. For example, it didn't stop a Barack from marrying a Michelle. But it has slowed us down some.

After slavery, the U.S. government promised Blacks 40 acres of land each (one acre is close to the size of a football field), so we could grow our own food and make money. But then the government changed its mind and gave us nothing. The violence and terror against Blacks was continued with beatings, rapings and lynchings by White terrorists, sometimes in organized groups like the Ku Klux Klan. They were afraid the newly freed Blacks would gain economic and political power. So for the next several decades Blacks were denied access to fair education and employment, making it hard for families to survive.

The entire United States history is full of examples of White Americans attacking Black people and Black people fighting back. A hundred years ago, the problem of Black poverty inspired solutions by Marcus Garvey who organized a movement to give Black people pride and economic independence. But it was still illegal to vote and get a fair education, which created the Ella Bakers, Martin Kings, Rosa Parks', Angela Davis', Stokely Carmichaels, and Malcolm X's.

Then church bombings, police brutality, and angry White mobs inspired a Black Panther Party to move beyond giving free breakfast to school children to talk more about self defense.

Then the government used its resources to destroy the Panthers and other organizations with secret FBI spy programs like COINTELPRO. So the holiday Kwanzaa was created, along with Black cultural schools and business. Then someone(s) began attacking Black communities with heroine and crack cocaine. Which created positive hip-hop. Then prisons. Then The Cosby Show. Then gentrification. Then we elected half a black president.

Black people have always fought. We continue to. And there is always some system, typically run by White people, ready to attack.

What do people mean when they say "the system" is against Black families?

My parents' generation used to complain about "The Man" attacking Black people. They were talking about oppressive institutions, symbolized by the face of a White man. These days you might hear people say "the system" instead. Either way they are talking about corporations, policies and values that have been in the United States since the founding fathers signed the Declaration of Independence. It can be too overwhelming to think about oppression coming from a giant system of constant attack. And it gives White people too much power to call them "devils". It's not that simple. There have been White allies fighting for justice and dying alongside Black people. Plus, these days there are Black people operating some of the institutions in "the systems" that are causing problems for Black families.

So what is this "system"? And what is it made of? Let's break it down into some of its parts. That way we can see it more clearly. "The system" is made up of large sections that can each be broken down into smaller sections. For example, let's look at the category of media. Media has the power to create and distribute images and ideas to billions of people. It has used that power to show persistent images of Black people as criminals and unintelligent. And it has neglected to promote images of loving and productive Black families.

If someone says "the media is the problem in our society" you should wonder exactly what they mean by media, because it includes lots of different parts. Let's break media down into some of its smaller categories:

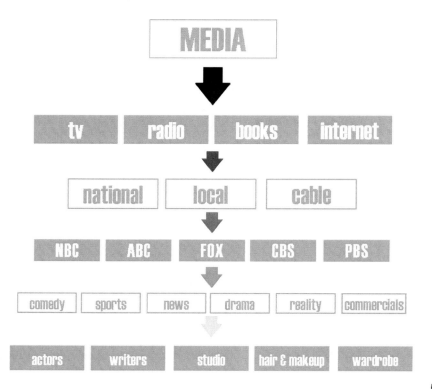

You get the idea right? Each part of the system can be broken down into its smallest parts, which is always people. You will always eventually find individual decision making human beings at the top and bottom of all these systems. These people are connected in a network of values and priorities that keep the American engine running.

Here are some other parts of the system that have caused problems for Black families:

ECONOMICS

Name ten companies or businesses, any kind...
(for example: United Airlines, Polo, Bank of America, Target, Google, Applebee's, Ford, Coca-Cola, Apple, Nike)

Now, name ten companies or businesses owned by White Americans...
(...United Airlines, Polo, Bank of America, Target, Google, Applebee's, Ford, Coca-Cola, Apple, Nike)

Hmm, notice any similarities?

Okay, now name ten black owned businesses...
(...can't think of any? How about BET? Or maybe Essence Magazine? Nope. Both of those have White owners)

Black people stay complaining about not having any power and what other people do to us but we are always the first to give all of our money away. A dollar circulates in Asian communities for a month, in Jewish communities approximately 20 days and white communities 17 days. In the Black community a dollar is gone in 6 hours. [13]

Walk around any neighborhood where a lot of Black people live and find out who owns the businesses there. In most places you might find a restaurant, some barber shops and hair salons that are black owned, but that's it. Almost everything else will be owned by people of other races, that don't live in the community. We could solve most if not all of our problems if we invested all of our money and resources in our own people. Every city that has a Chinatown should also have a Blacktown.

HEALTH

While you're walking around Black low-income neighborhoods also take note of the food available there. There's probably no grocery store in walking distance. So the only options will be corner stores, with candy, soda (or 'pop' if you where I'm from), Flaming Hots, and maybe a few vegetables. You'll see a lot of fried fast food. Liquor and weed will be easy to find.

If you wanted to feed your kids healthy, organic, fresh food, you probably won't be able to find it, unless you go to neighborhoods where more White people live.

LAW

American laws are based on the Constitution. Some of the men that wrote the Constitution were White terrorists who enslaved Africans. When they wrote "We the people..." they weren't talking about you.

Many laws give White Americans an unfair advantage. Some of those laws were created to make sure you and other young Black men get stuck in the prison system. And these laws are enforced by police officers who sometimes abuse their power by hurting and killing weaponless people.

There's a recent book called ***The New Jim Crow: Mass Incarceration in the Age of Colorblindness***, by the lawyer Michelle Alexander, about how the law is unfairly used against Black people.

RELIGION

If we were being completely honest, we'd admit that when we close our eyes tight, and think about what God looks like—or if you're Christian, what Jesus looks like—the image that usually pops up first is a White man.

> *"A people will never be free when they worship a god assigned to them and they can never respect a black Father in the home when they have a white Father hanging on the wall."*
> —Dr. John Henrik Clarke

There is nothing wrong with religion. They all have beautiful messages of peace, love and service. Plus, the most popular religions have origins in Africa (as explained in the book *African Origins of the Major "Western Religions"* by Dr. Yosef Ben-Jochannan). There is, however, something wrong with forcing religions onto people, which usually happens to the most vulnerable people. And there is something wrong with changing religious text and interpretation to fit the political agenda of the rich and powerful.

EDUCATION

Most schools are designed to train students to become effective employees. Schools don't teach how to think, they teach what to think. Most of what you need to know about your culture, history, and the skills to create and maintain families and businesses will not be taught in most schools.

The trick to using school to your advantage is learning to play it like a game. Doing well at school can be very helpful for making money and being successful in this world. It's important to gain the language, skills, organization, and discipline that school offers. You just have to be careful to not take all the information there as the ultimate truth. There are lots of times when your teachers will tell obvious lies. For example: "Greeks were the fathers of math and science" or "the native Americans were savages". In most schools you start the day, hand on your heart pledging allegiance to the US flag. Many schools will celebrate your athletic talents before they encourage your intellectual gifts. They might try to make you feel dumb, but ignore them. Don't use school to validate your worth. Work hard anyway. Not to prove anybody wrong, but because YOU benefit from learning how to play the game well.

MEDIA

Before TV and internet, the only media around was books. That's how information was shared around the world. Some of White people's greatest scholars have used books to write terrible and false things about Black people. For example, scientist Francis Galton, in 1873, wrote: "Average Negros possess too little intellect, self-reliance, and self-control to make it possible for them to sustain the burden of any respectable form of civilization without a large measure of guidance and support."

Later, through radio and TV, Black people were ignored or worse. The popular ways to represent Black people have been: 1) as dumb [to justify taking us out of Africa, as if we couldn't take care of ourselves] or 2) dangerous and aggressive [to justify White people controlling us] and 3) constantly craving sex [to justify all the sexual abuse White people forced onto Black people].

Today, Black people create and support these same destructive images of ourselves. You can find all the same characters in popular rap videos: Black people looking dumb, aggressive and overly sexual. We think we're doing something new. But we're doing the same thing racist White people used to do. Let's take, for example, the big booty half naked video vixen you see in most rap videos. She is just a modern version of Saartjie Baartman.

Saartjie Baartman was a woman from South Africa in the 1800s who had large breasts and butt. Some White people went to her hometown and took her to Europe to make money by putting her body on display. She was also examined by scientists. One of them said, "the three men had great difficulty in convincing Sarah [they changed her name] to let herself be seen nude. It was only with great sorrow that she let drop for a moment, the handkerchief, with which she had been covering her genitals. At one point he offered her money, knowing how much she liked it, hoping in this way to render her more docile. But she refused to take it." [14] Black men should be outraged when we see women treated like that.

I love hip-hop. I think it's brilliant. We gotta be honest though about why some of it causes so many problems for Black people. I wanna call some names out right now. Or talk about some specific songs and lyrics that are really harmful. But that won't even matter, because the names will change. There's always gonna be new dumb songs to complain about. There will always be cowards willing to say anything for money. Television and radio have the power of repetition. So even if you don't like a dumb song at first, by the time they play it 50 times you'll find yourself nodding your head on beat without even thinking about it. Without ever listening to the words they're saying.

The problem really isn't what rappers say. The problem is that we believe them. We think they really spend all their time thinking about drugs, cars, jewelry and sex. But that's a lie. They're real people, with real feelings. And friendships. And children. And parents. And worries. And dreams. But they don't rap about any of that because the radio won't play it. And a lot of them don't have the courage to be honest.

SIDENOTE: There are lots of honest, very smart, productive hip-hop artists in the world. They need us to find them and support their stuff.

We should listen to some rappers just like we watch actors in a movie. We don't assume Denzel Washington, in real life, acts like the cop he pretended to be in Training Day. We should see rappers in the same way. Even though they want you to think they are 'keeping it real', they're lying. Rappers have teams of people that write their lyrics, and dress them, and give them women and cars to borrow. It's all pretend.

How do we use history to move forward?

I always hate to see when young Black men play the role that was created for them by the European terrorists that brought us here during slavery and the racist Whites who want us to stay enslaved. Too many Black men fall right into the traps. Chasing money, then giving it right back to White businesses. Selling drugs that destroy communities. Fighting and killing each other. Treating women like shit. Abandoning our children. Thinking that education, reading, being intelligent and being healthy is White people stuff. It all breaks my heart every time. I always think about our ancestors. Those Africans who made the ultimate sacrifice, to survive under constant terror with only the hope that their children might have a better life.

Next, I think about our African history before slavery, all the powerful civilizations we built. And I wonder if Black men would still be filling up prisons if we knew how brilliant we are. Marcus Garvey said "what humans have done, humans can do." So I have confidence in Black people's ability to contribute amazing things to this world, not because it sounds good to say, but because it has already happened.

It's important to use history to find identity. Everybody should do that. Mexicans should learn about the heritage and history of Mexico. Chinese should learn about the heritage and history of China, and so on. Blacks have had a hard time doing that because we've been lied to about Africa for so long. I find power in African culture. In the music, the languages, the clothes, the food, the values, and the people of Africa. For me, it's one way to fight against the European terrorists that enslaved us. They tried to make us forget about where we came from and to hate our culture. We can't let them win that battle.

Finally, I think about history and how powerful Black people have been because of how strong our families have been. It makes me sad to see so many couples struggling and fighting each other. We make enemies out of each other, even though we have real enemies. I'm sad thinking about how many children have to figure out how to make it in this tough world without help from the man AND the woman that brought them here. Because the adults can't work out their relationship stuff, or even try to get along as friends. So that is why it's really important for us to have more serious conversations about ways to find, create and build healthy relationships with each other.

CHAPTER 3
HOW DO WE CREATE HEALTHY RELATIONSHIPS?

I'm your Mister, you my Mrs., with hugs and kisses. Valentine cards and birthday wishes?? Please. Be on another level of planning, of understanding the bond between man and woman, and child. The highest elevation. 'Cause we above all that romance crap, just show your love. –Method Man

What do Malcolm X, Martin Luther King, Nelson Mandela, and Barack Obama have in common?

Betty, Coretta, Winnie, and Michelle.

These men will go down in history as some of the most powerful men ever. They were each able to reach success and impact the world <u>because</u> they had powerful women as partners. These women were their wives, not their wifeys, boo's, honey dips, or whatever we call them these days. And they were all dope women on their own, before they met their husbands.

There is only one way to be in the best relationship possible. Only one way to have the **bad**dest, **smart**est, **fly**est, prettiest, funniest girl interested in you. And that is… (drumroll)… you have to be *your* <u>best self first</u>! Ain't no way around it. You have to be the most successful, most disciplined, as intelligent, and as healthy as you can possibly be on your own.

Don't go looking for some woman to complete you. She can support you. She can encourage you. She can make you better. But it is not her job to make a man out of you.

Why am I starting the relationship chapter talking about you, as an individual? Shouldn't I be giving advice on how to meet and talk to women? But that's just it! That's the secret. You won't have to worry about <u>finding</u> the best woman if you're focused on <u>being</u> your best self. When you get more disciplined, smarter, more interesting and more successful, then you're more likely to <u>attract</u> the woman of your dreams. You won't need slick game, expensive clothes or fancy cars. All you will have to do is <u>be you</u>, and **she will just show up in your life**.

If you're always complaining about having too many "weak" girls around, then **that must be what you're attracting**. And complaining about the girls ain't gone solve that problem. We will talk more about what it means to be the best man possible in the next chapter. For now, let's talk about dating.

To get started, how do you choose the right girl to ask on a date?

Men waste a lot of time chasing women for the wrong reasons. Then, we finally do bump into a special lady, one we really care about, and won't know what to do! When you find a special one, you want to try your best to hold on to her. Otherwise you'll regret it forever.

A lot of guys go for the <u>shiny</u> girl. And by shiny I don't mean she uses too much cocoa butter. I mean the most popular girl, the center of attention. She thinks she's on a red carpet runway everywhere she goes. She wears fancy jewelry, the newest brand named clothes, her hair always did. She spends a lot of time thinking about her appearance. Dating her can be expensive because she's used to guys trying to impress her with money.

The shiny girl is different from the <u>substance</u> girl. The substance girl reads books. She has cool interests like travel, or poetry, martial arts, or astronomy. She might speak different languages. She has talents—dances, plays instruments, or writes plays. Sometimes she's a good student, but not necessarily. Conversations with the substance girl feel very different than with the shiny girl. After you talk with the substance girl you walk away still thinking about the conversation. The substance girl makes you look at the world differently.

Sometimes, if you're paying close attention, you will find the substance girl and the shiny girl in the **same** person. The most popular girl in school can also be smart, talented, and down to earth. The truth is you never really know what's inside a person, looking at them from the outside. T.I. said something like that in a song once:

> Now I been told every nigga in the streets know
> She ain't nothing but a freak ho
> But when I look in her pretty eyes, I don't see it though
> Now she done showed me some shit that I ain't seen before

(Disclaimer: I'm using this quote just to make this specific point. This is not an endorsement of T.I. He has said and done lots of problematic things that he needs to be accountable for.)

When you're open to meeting someone special, it matters less what other people think about her. It becomes easier to ignore whatever reputation a girl might have, because you're getting to learn who she really is. Plus, <u>you</u> might have your own reputation you want <u>her</u> to ignore.

Rapper 50-cent also wrote a song about dating. He raps questions to ask while getting to know a woman. In his lyrics he's worried about getting locked up, and probably not for fighting against injustice like a political prisoner. But it's still worth noticing when so-called gangsta rappers take a moment to talk about matters of the heart:

> If I got locked up and sentenced to a quarter century, could I count on you to be there to support me mentally?
> If I went back to a hoopty from a Benz, would you poof and disappear like some of my friends?
> Do you trust me enough, to tell me your dreams?

Going on actual dates

This is the best way to get to know a woman. Don't skip this part and try going right to her house to watch movies. Going on dates is your first chance to show her how you treat someone you care about. Take her somewhere fun and interesting. Pay for the date (which doesn't mean she owes you anything). Open her doors. Pull her chair out before she sits down. Ask her questions about her family, her dreams and her favorite things to do. Find out what makes her smile.

You don't want to spend your last dollar on a date though. If you're broke, you just have to be more creative. There's usually free stuff to do. Free festivals, movies or music in the park, free museum days, etc. Just get on the internet and do a little research, or find a free community newspaper that lists events. You can also make up something to do. Take a train or bus into a brand new neighborhood, take a walk, find interesting people to watch, or volunteer on a service project together. Be creative. Be thoughtful. Try to impress her.

And don't be fake. If you don't like poetry, don't go on a date to a poetry slam and pretend like you all into it. Don't walk into the room hi-fiving strangers like you be there every week. However, it can be a good idea to plan something you wouldn't typically do or something you think she would like. Dating is a good way for both of you to find new & interesting things to get into.

Treat dating like an adventure. You'll learn a lot about yourself, and the woman you're dating. You wanna see if yall enjoy the same kinds of stuff. Go to a comedy show, find out if the same things make you laugh. You also want to see if she appreciates the effort you're showing. It's really important though, especially in the beginning, to be kind and giving **without expecting anything in return**.

Most of what I'm suggesting I learned from my father, who learned from his father. It's the "old fashioned" way we learn to be gentleman. But these actions: paying for a woman, opening her doors, etc. come from a time when men also tried to dominate woman. That's not what this is about. The point of relationships IS NOT to find someone that submits to you, that you can control. Good relationships are partnerships. Everyone is considered an equal. You might have different skills, sometimes the man is a better cook than the woman, sometimes the woman is better at keeping up with the money than the man. You just have to figure out what works for you, and don't get caught up in anybody else's ideas about what role a man or a woman is supposed to play in *your* relationship.

Inter-racial dating

Come on, you didn't really think I was gonna ignore this did you? If you'd rather date White girls or other races, you certainly have that right. But this is a thinking book, so I just want us to think for a moment about where the preference for non-Black girls might come from.

Sometimes love can be mysterious. It'll sneak up on you when you least expect it. Other times that shit is real predictable. When you see something over and over again you gotta start to wonder. Like when Black men get rich or famous and <u>then</u> start showing up with a White girl on their arm, looking proud like they finally get to live the American dream.

It's no secret that White men own most of the TV stations, movie studios, and magazines—all the places that control images. So it makes sense that they would glamorize their own women as the most beautiful and most desirable. It becomes a problem, though, when Black men also see these images and become <u>more</u> attracted to White women than Black women. Do these men think their own mothers, grandmothers, aunts, and sisters are less beautiful?

Sometimes it's not about dating actual White women. Some guys develop an attraction for only "White women features". The first guys breakin' they neck to look at the light skinned girl with long straight hair <u>be the same guys</u> telling women they're crazy for getting plastic surgery to make their nose thinner, and for risking their health with skin bleaching or hair straightening chemicals.

Black women with naturally light skin and straight hair are <u>in no way</u> any less Black than dark skinned kinky haired women. Black people are very diverse, so there is lots of variety in what Blackness means and looks like. The point is, all women deserve to be appreciated and admired for the natural beauty they all possess, just as God or Nature created them.

<u>Compatibility</u>

A good relationship is like a good team. They work together, support each other, have fun, and give something valuable back to the world. Watching an All-Star game reminds me of how important compatibility is for a team. In an All-Star game you have the best players from around the league, playing together maybe for the first time. The game may be fun to watch because the top athletes are all showing off. But sometimes they look awkward together. Even though the All-Star teams have the best individual players, they haven't had the time to develop into a good team. A solid playing regular team might beat an All-Star team. Because a solid team will have routine plays they can run whenever they need to, they know each other's strengths and weaknesses, and will have developed chemistry. No amount of individual talent can replace good rhythm or experience working together.

The whole point of dating is to learn what works for you. You wanna learn what you like, and what women like about you. We have to figure out who matches us the best. Which can be different for each person. It might also change over time. But that's what compatibility means, two people fit each other. We all have things about ourselves that we need to work on. No one is perfect. But we might have a part of our personality that one person sees as a flaw, that another person sees as a good thing.

Unfortunately, there's no magic formula for this part. It's all trial and error. You just gotta get out there, take risks, share yourself genuinely, maybe get hurt a couple of times, but keep on moving. It's all worth it though, when you find yourself ready to be committed, and with a woman that gets you in a way that nobody else does.

If you have decided to be in a committed relationship, how do you make it work?

Step 1: Define COMMITMENT

I used to be really bad at this part. I would be real comfortable keeping girls in that "grey area" space. Where we're kinda together, but not really, but sometimes. Those set-ups are hard because no one knows the cheating rules. And I'd always get 'caught' and be like, *"But what had happened was, we wasn't really together together, so I thought it was cool..."* The "grey area" is a selfish way of trying to hold on to a woman without really committing to her. A lot of drama can be avoided with clarity.

SIDENOTE: This step is also a really good time to make sure your attraction to a woman is meant to be romantic. Authentic interactions with people can be so rare that as soon as we feel a connection with a woman we automatically figure it means date her. But sometimes it could mean you're supposed to be really close friends, which can be even more intimate and meaningful. Don't ruin that by pushing a physical or romantic relationship.

You want to get off to a good start. Make sure you're ready. Then make a clear agreement. Say out loud you want to date each other exclusively. That means don't date any other girls. Claim each other publicly. Change your Facebook status. Tell the other women in your life. Tell the other women in your life. Give her the same respect you expect from her. Don't pretend to commit if you don't want to. If you're not ready, if you want to date other people, or if you don't believe in monogamy, that's fine. Just don't lie about it. Even if it means you lose access to some of her.

But if you're serious, and honestly ready, then there's much to enjoy about healthy relationships.

Step 2: Add ingredients of a healthy relationship

We're supposed to learn how to be in relationships from our parents. It's not something we automatically know how to do. A lot of people struggle in relationships because they never learned how to be in them. You would be a bad driver, a bad cook, a bad lawyer....a bad <u>anything</u>, if no one ever teaches you how. It's always harder when you learn by making it up as you go along. Or by relying on peers that have also not been taught.

Nature/God's design was brilliant. Two people come together, and make a new person. They're supposed to take care of the persons they create. We're not doing that. But if that plan worked, we'd all learn how to be in relationships by watching our parents. We'd just imitate their success. And avoid their mistakes. Each generation would naturally get better and better at it.

I haven't been married yet. But I have been in a few relationships. I've been a counselor to couples, I've read a bunch of books about relationships, and I've spent years looking for examples of relationships to watch and study.

What I've learned so far is there are lots of different ways couples work. However, there are several <u>ingredients</u> that most successful relationships have in common.

1. Love

I feel like I should say something beautiful here. Like poetry. But I don't really think about **love** like that. Sometimes, I actually think that romantic stuff can get in the way of genuine intimacy. For example, a guy can get away with buying the same ol' chocolate and flowers for his girlfriend and never really pay attention to what she actually likes.

The rush of <u>love's beginning</u> is an important part of the process. That's when yall first meet and she is the most amazing, beautiful and magical woman that has ever walked the Earth. Even her mistakes are golden. When yall spend one second apart it feels like you can't breathe. As much fun as it is, this part fades away. And when the excitement calms, after you've already promised her your eternal heart, you will both find yourselves having to figure out if yall really **like** each other. If yall can still talk about careers, children and chores. You gotta see if your families can get along. And if you really love each other's mean, ugly, and embarrassing parts.

I like my **love** more practical. Sure, it's nice to hear someone <u>tell</u> <u>you</u> they love you sometimes but it's always better when they <u>show</u> it. When anyone tells me "I love you" the response in my head is always: *Oh yeah, where? I want to see it.* You can keep all the pretty words and love songs if you <u>act</u> like you love me. **Love should have evidence.**

A lot of Black men get backwards ideas about love from the music we listen to. Women are a popular topic in rap music, but usually not in healthy ways. When the topic of love comes up, rappers often get it wrong. Sometimes rappers get confused and think love is something you can <u>buy</u>:

A month ago, I gave a chick a hundred stacks
Straight to Neiman Marcus, young bitch had a heart attack
Aww man, I love my bitches.

—Rick Ross

Another common mistake is to say love is the same thing as <u>sex</u>. Rappers also confuse love with <u>control</u>. Here's a verse that does both at the same time:

Oh yes I love her, like her dad told her no man would ever love her
Oh and I better be the only man stickin' it
Lickin' it like an envelope, mailin' it, sealin' it
Read it, I have written down Victoria's Secret
Don't tell nobody, don't share your body with nobody
Not even a finger, I will cut it off and let him keep it

—Lil Wayne

The **love = power** confusion is something Black men need to be extra careful about. Especially as we become more aware of being in the world with limited social, economic and political power. Because we'll be out living life, going through the day, watching men of other races enjoy their power. Then when we are at home with the women we love, we try to re-gain our own feelings of power by dominating our relationships. For example, we might speak to a girlfriend or a wife aggressively, or walk in the house demanding they cook or clean. Or we might try to control their friendships or activities. What makes it worse, is that we do it all in the name of love! We get confused and think controlling women is how we show we care.

I wonder sometimes if misunderstood lessons from religion contribute to this confusion. (Since religion is also how we learn what love means.)We are taught that God has all power and control, and He loves us deeply. But we should fear Him because He will punish us if we don't believe or praise Him enough. Something seems strange to me about that kind of love.

Okay, so… love is _not_ sex, and it is _not_ money, or romance, or control, or power…. then what _is_ it? Well, I hate to disappoint, but there's no good answer to that question. Love is just one of those things. You could have a thousand people define love a thousand different ways. They'd all be right AND you'd still be missing the essence of it. Figuring out what love is for you is a part of the adventure of relationships. Because you know when you've found it. Remember, when love comes in your life, there's always evidence.

Part of it is a feeling, but there's usually more. When you find someone you love and they love you back, then something changes. You might walk a little taller, or laugh more, or be more productive, or discover new talents. And if you're not paying attention you may have found love, but don't realize it until you lose it. Then, you will feel the difference when she's gone. And when that happens, you better hope it's not too late.

As powerful as **love** is, two people loving each other is usually not enough to keep a relationship together for a long time. You're gonna need a few more ingredients to keep a relationship healthy. Love in relationships works a lot like hope - it's not enough to build your whole life on, but life without it, isn't much of a life at all.

2. Communication

This is the glue that holds relationships together. OR it is the hammer that breaks them apart. If there was any section that I would've wanted to write a whole book about, it would be the communication section. ← That was a waste of a sentence. I'm worried about not being able to say enough about communication and I used some of that space to complain about how I wish I could say more. Oh crap, I did it again! I'm just kidding. I did that on purpose. To make my first point: **you can say lots of words without really communicating anything**.

A better title for this section would be Good Communication or Effective Communication. The goal is to have a message or idea, and pass it on like a football, to be received exactly as it was intended. A dropped ball could be the quarterback's fault for throwing it too hard or too soft. Or it could be the receiver's fault for not paying attention. Or both. But a **successful** catch always takes both the thrower and the receiver being in sync. Also, in relationships there are often linebacker-sized obstacles, trying to block good communication.

You ever said something stupid that you had to take back later? We say things we don't mean sometimes. Stuff just kinda just slips out of our mouths. The very first step in communicating well is one that people often overlook: **figure out <u>what it is</u> you have to say**. Which doesn't always happen immediately. It certainly doesn't happen when we're angry. So this first step *'figure out what you have to say'* sometimes means you should walk away from the conversation for a moment. And breathe. And carefully figure out what you are feeling and thinking. A lot of miscommunication could be avoided if we took more time to first decide what is important to say, before we start running our mouth.

[Tip: Writing down what you want to say first may help.]

After you have a clear message to communicate, then the next step is to decide **how to communicate** it. There are lots of different ways to express an idea. The two main categories are <u>verbal</u> and <u>nonverbal</u>. *Verbal communication* is when you say the best words you can think of to express an idea. (Having a good vocabulary can help improve verbal communication.) *Non-verbal communication* uses actions, like hand movements, facial expressions, closeness /distance, or gestures like buying gifts. This is also known sometimes as body language. Let's look at a few examples. For each of the following ideas or <u>messages</u>, I'm gonna share some verbal and non-verbal options for communicating them.

MESSAGE #1: I AM VERY HAPPY WITH YOU TODAY. THIS RELATIONSHIP IS AMAZING!

VERBAL COMMUNICATION:	Say:
	"I am very happy with you today. This relationship is amazing."
	OR
	"I really appreciate you."
	OR
	"You're a wonderful woman. I'm so glad we met."
	OR
	"This is the best thing that ever happened to me."
	OR
	"I can't believe this is so good. I'm the luckiest man on the planet to have you by my side."
NON-VERBAL COMMUNICATION:	Smile when she comes in the door. Hug, kiss, or touch her softly. Do something special for her like cook a special meal. Take her out somewhere fun. Plan an activity in the house that she likes to do. Serve her. Clean her space. Give her a massage. Buy her a surprise gift.

MESSAGE #2: I HAD A TERRIBLE DAY TODAY AND I NEED SOME SPACE.

VERBAL COMMUNICATION:	Say:
	"I had a terrible day today and I need some space."
	OR
	"I'm not feeling well. Let me get a few minutes alone."
	OR
	"Now's not a good time. We can talk later."
	OR
	"I love you, and I promise I'm not mad at you. You did nothing wrong. I just need some time by myself."
NON-VERBAL COMMUNICATION:	Walk in the house, politely kiss her on the cheek and quickly walk into another room, sit down and turn on the TV or open up a book.
	OR
	Move slowly, with a sad expression on your face so she can see that you look upset.
	OR
	If you're not ready to be around anyone, make an extra stop at the park and walk it off, or drive around for a while before you go home.

MESSAGE #3: I HAD A TERRIBLE DAY TODAY AND I NEED SOME ATTENTION.

VERBAL COMMUNICATION:	Say: "I had a terrible day today and I need some attention." OR "I'm not feeling that good. Can we talk or go do something fun?" OR "I know you might be busy right now, but I really need you. Could I borrow a few minutes of your time?" OR "I'm having the worst day. I could really use some help feeling better."
NON-VERBAL COMMUNICATION:	Walk or move slowly, with your head down, and a sad facial expression, and go over to her and put your arms around her. OR Sit next to her on a couch and gently grab her arm and pull her over to you. OR Walk over to wherever she is and lay your head on her shoulder or on her lap.

MESSAGE #4: I'M NOT HAPPY WITH THE WAY YOU DID SOMETHING.

VERBAL COMMUNICATION:	Say: "I'm not happy with the way you did that." OR "When you say or do things like that, it makes me feel like you don't care." OR "I really wish you wouldn't talk to me or treat me like that." OR "I'm not sure how much I'd be okay staying in this relationship with you if you keep doing that." OR "Maybe you didn't mean it, but it hurts me when you say (or do) that."
NON-VERBAL COMMUNICATION:	When you're with her don't make eye contact or touch her. OR Stay away from her completely. Don't answer the phone or respond to texts. [Tip: Don't ignore for too long. Women hate that. And don't ignore to avoid difficult conversations either. I'm just saying it's okay to give yourself space to gather your thoughts if you need to.]

There are <u>so</u> <u>many</u> ways to communicate. You are constantly delivering messages in relationships. The **clothes** you wear say something. The **music** you play while a girl is at your house sends a message. If you always show up late someone might think it means you don't really care. Or if you show up early **all the time** it could be viewed as being too eager. You could even show up exactly on time every time and someone may think you are too stiff and rigid.

Even NOT communicating is communicating. If someone calls you five times and you ignore it, you have sent them the message *I don't want to talk to you right now* without saying anything. Or you ask your lady a question, like "Do you still love me?" and she says nothing. If she just sits there quietly staring at the ground, that may be all the information you need. Sometimes silence in relationships can be louder than any words.

And after ALL that, sometimes we have to accept that a message we want to send will NOT be received. You can desperately want to express a thought or feeling to someone and they may never get it. They might not want to get it. They might not be ready to understand. And you have to learn to be okay with that.

<u>Listening</u>

So now, after reading this far we have become experts in communication! Congratulations... right? Nope. Sorry. We have only just been talking about <u>one</u> <u>half</u> of the communication process. You can try your hardest to say something as clearly as possible. You can make great efforts figuring out the best way to express your sincerest thoughts and feelings. But **you have no control over what the other person hears or sees**.

We all see the world from our own perspective. Like individually tailored glasses. Everyone hears information <u>through</u> their own brain. Imagine I'm having a conversation with a woman. The words start in my brain, which is a machine that has been developing for 30 plus years. And my brain has had its own experiences with love, joy and pain. The words come out of my mouth, float through the air, into her ears, to finally be understood by her brain. I have no idea how my words are going to be <u>received</u> in her brain. I could say one word, like 'trust', and it instantly reminds her of 15 **different** experiences she's had with the word 'trust'. Some good, some bad, but all different from the experiences I had with <u>trust</u>.

The best way to find out if she understands <u>what I mean</u>, is to ask her. *"I think you might have misunderstood me. Can you please say back to me what you heard me say?"* Or say *"You have a funny look on your face. Maybe I said that wrong."* And you don't necessarily want your exact words repeated, you just want to hear if she understood you. If she's right, then you say *"Well, yeah. That's exactly what I meant"* (which means that funny look on her face is a whole new issue). Or if she says something back that wasn't really what you meant, then it's **your responsibility** to figure out a different way to say it.

The skill we're talking about is good <u>listening</u>. Learning to be a good listener is, at least, as important as being a good talker. Listening takes patience and an open mind. Good listening is a critical part of being in good relationships. It shows your partner that you care about who she is. On a really basic level, listening to each other is the way we remind the people we love that they're not in the world alone. That they matter, in that moment, to at least one person.

<u>Arguing</u>

There's nothing wrong with arguing, sometimes. Conflict is a natural part of life, and relationships. Each conflict usually brings a unique opportunity to learn something or grow in important ways. (If the conflict is dealt with in the right way.) So don't avoid it. But also, **fight fair**. When you're arguing with a woman, make sure you're still listening to what she is saying. Don't just have a yelling match, cause then nobody's listening to nobody. Don't use the argument to say something hurtful that you'll regret later. And if she makes points during an argument that are true, then pause and give her credit. (*"Yeah, you right, that's true."*) Don't let your pride get in the way. The point of the conflict is NOT to win the argument. The goal is to resolve the problem.

And if you're upset, **never become physically aggressive**. Only weak men try to use their strength to threaten a woman. Even if you never touch her, stuff like punching the wall or throwing things is a weak man's way of intimidating a woman by reminding her of his physical strength.

3. Mutual Benefit

The next ingredient to a healthy relationship is pretty easy. Both people should get something out of the relationship. Give and give. You shouldn't be together for a year <u>and neither of you</u> is any different than when you met. Or if <u>just one of you</u> has been learning and growing and enjoying the other, that won't work either. Relationships need balance.

The best way to achieve **mutual benefit** is to have two people come into the relationship with the goal of contributing something valuable to the other. If you're both making an effort <u>to give</u> to the other <u>at the same time</u> then neither of you will have to worry about being taken advantage of.

4. Compromise

Sometimes relationships are like live music, when the performer gives more, the audience gets more excited. The <u>performer + audience</u> combo gives itself energy, and both parts benefit instantly (<u>mutual benefit</u>). Other times relationships are like a see-saw. When one person is up, the other is down. This is **compromise**. Give and take. Over time you want your relationship to end up looking 50/50, with an equal amount of give and take. But in some moments it'll look more 80/20. You might be in a good place and can give 80% of your time, energy, or attention to her, while she's temporarily giving 20%. Then later you switch.

The secret to **compromise** in your relationship is being able to <u>sacrifice</u>. You can't always have everything you want. You may have to do things or go places that you don't feel like.

Do them anyway. When you live alone you can do whatever you like. But when you live with your lady, you might have to keep your Scarface poster in the basement, or clean up more, or limit your visitors. If the relationship does not have <u>mutual</u> <u>benefit</u> then **compromise** can feel like you're giving up some of your freedom. But when it's a healthy relationship, then you will gain freedom from the security and support of the partnership.

5. Intimacy

A lot of men hear the word 'intimacy' and think sex. But that's only a small part of it. **Intimacy** is really about sharing personal and genuine moments with someone else. There's so much fake in the world that it's nice to meet a woman you can be completely real with, without judgment. When you have intimacy with someone, you can share your deepest secrets. You <u>accept</u> each other in the most honest way.

When you are with someone you love, and you both feel safe, <u>after a while</u> yall may decide to express that intimacy physically, with sex. **Which is a very big deal decision**. Having sex just because it feels good is <u>not</u> worth the risks. If you just want pleasure, you're better off taking care of it on your own. You can't give yourself herpes.

Sex makes children. Every time you think about maybe having sex with a woman you must <u>always</u> think two things: 1) Am I ready to have children? And 2) Do I want to have a child with **this** woman? If you're not sure about either of those answers, then don't do it.

[Tip: condoms are cheaper than children.]

6. Trust

It's almost impossible to stay in a relationship with someone you don't trust. And trust is tricky. The reason you don't trust someone could <u>because of **them**</u>, or it could be <u>because of **you**</u>. If you find yourself checking her phone, using her password, or not believing her, then you've got to ask yourself "why?". Is it because some **other** woman lied or cheated before, and you're trying to protect yourself from being hurt again? Or is it because you've already caught the current woman lying or cheating on you?

I give everyone 100% trust at all times, until they show me something different. I don't like sneaking through texts or inbox messages. I think people should have privacy. If I suspect a woman is cheating on me, then I'll come straight out and ask her. Because if she finds out I'm checking her phone, then she'll just get sneakier and start deleting messages. If she wants to be with another man, then she'll just leave eventually. Until then, I always assume she's telling the truth. Not trusting her is too much stress for me.

If you actually catch a woman cheating on you, you may decide to stay in the relationship anyway. If that's true, then you must really <u>forgive</u> her. And then, still, there's no reason to go checking her phone. If she cheats again, you'll eventually find out. And if you can't genuinely trust her again, then maybe the relationship should end.

This also goes both ways. If you want trust in the relationship, you have to make sure you're not doing anything with other women that violates the rules. If you meet someone else, or want to start dating other people, then just get out of the relationship.

Yes, I know. I make all this sound so easy. In real life I know this is all a little more difficult. I'm not saying I ain't never checked a girl's phone before. But I do think relationships could be less complicated than we make them.

Relationships should make us feel safe. There should be space to be genuine and vulnerable. That's how the personal growth happens. The world is dangerous and unpredictable. Purposefully creating **trusting relationships** is one way to have at least one thing we can depend on.

What is the Best Way to End Relationships?

We live in a microwave society. We like things fast and convenient. Relationships don't work like that. The attraction can happen fast, but getting to know each other and learning how to work together takes time. Too many people quit at the first sign of trouble. We're not patient enough to push through the natural discomfort of turning two into one. And since people aren't gonna stop having sex, it's really the kids who suffer from adults not being able to figure out how to stay in relationships.

The hardest decision to make in a relationship is knowing when to either walk away or try harder. Sometimes forcing yourself to stay in a relationship is a really bad idea. Some couples are just not a good fit. Partners can even bring out the worst in each other. If you are being physically or emotionally abused, then you definitely need to go. But if you're not happy, or not being appreciated, or always giving to someone who's just taking, or feel stuck, or bored, etc. then there's more to think about.

You should not stay for the wrong reasons, like if you're just afraid of being lonely. But you also shouldn't leave for the wrong reasons either. Some people want to break up just to have a fresh start with someone new. They assume they can find someone better and might have somebody else in mind already. They forget that the newness fades, every time. And with each person there's gonna be stuff you don't like and will have to learn to deal with.

You also don't want to end a relationship because you're scared of commitment. Because you still wanna play around and date random women. And you don't wanna leave at the first difficult moment in a relationship. **Make sure you give it your best try first**. Talk to her. Try to see if yall can come up with some solutions to your problems. Then be patient and see if those solutions work. You and/or she may need to make some changes in your habits or personality. Those take time. And if yall need help, there's nothing wrong with that. Every successful couple I know has gotten help along the way. So go to a counselor. Talk to a minister, priest, or imam. Find some elders or successful couples in your family or community, and talk to them.

After all that, if you still decide you want to end a relationship then you want to do it right. Be honest. Say why. Give the woman space afterwards if that's what she asks for. Don't continue to be physical with her and pretend like it's okay cause you already told her it was over. Don't start dating another woman until you make a clean, clear break with the first woman. And if she's upset and says hurtful things to you, then just take it. Don't fight back. Just walk away respectfully. And **take some space after relationships, for yourself, to be alone**. Learn from the old relationship before you jump into another one.

Alright, let's end this chapter with a few Do's and Don'ts. Some clear rules for relationships that may have gotten lost in the sections above.

ALWAYS DO

1. *Say what you mean. And mean what you say.* Be honest. I can't say that enough. Just be honest. Don't coward out of moments to be genuine or vulnerable.

2. *Treat women like you'd want a man to treat your sister/ daughter/mother.* We should treat people right just because. That should be how humans naturally operate. But it's also good karma. Everything's connected. When you treat women like trash it shows other men that it's okay. Eventually, maintaining a trash standard will get back around to the women you love. Your cousins, little sisters and your own daughter. Some man will the do the exact same thing to your daughter that you did to women. Unless you show them better.

3. *Learn from your mistakes. And other people's mistakes.* We all mess up. The only way to make up for it is to learn from it. Feeling guilty, and apologizing, and beating yourself up about it, don't mean nothing if you keep repeating the same old mistakes. Seek advice from older men. Your father, uncles, coaches, ministers, teachers, etc. But remember,

they're not perfect either. They've also made mistakes, so ask them to be honest about them.

4. ***Find examples.*** To get good at basketball, you watch better basketball players. It's the same thing with relationships. You have to find other couples that work. You can usually tell when a couple is happy together. Find them and spend time around them.

5. ***Protect women.*** Yes, women are very strong and can protect themselves. They can also open their own doors and carry their own groceries, but when you're around, she shouldn't have to. Protecting women doesn't mean she's weaker than you, or give you the right to control her. It just means that you have a specific role on the team, to make sure that everyone is safe. You should do anything you can to create a safe environment in your home, church, and community. No man, woman or child should ever be afraid of being sexually or physically harmed.

This also means protecting them from the violence and insult from the music and images that get repeated over and over on the TV and radio. It's better to think about protecting girls (and also boys) that are younger that you. So if you are 16, for example, then you want to get rid of the harmful images and words in the media that a 7 year old will be exposed to. Another 16 year old young lady can protect herself.

Just bleeping out curse words isn't enough. At least, we have to stop supporting the stuff that hurts us. And at most, we have to go to the stations that play it, and the corporations that create it, and stop them.

6. ***Ask an older man you respect to add a few more to this list.***

_____

_____

NEVER DO

1. ***Don't collect women who like you just to fill in the gaps of your dislike for yourself.*** Avoid the urge to invite women over or hang out with them just because you're lonely. Part of being mature is learning how to be alone. You should be able to sit a quiet room alone and be perfectly happy.

2. ***Don't take advantage of, pressure or manipulate women.*** You have been trained to treat women like toys since before you can remember. Watch what people do with a baby boy, call him 'lil playa' and call him a 'heartbreaker'. You have to reject that training.

   You only want to do things with a woman that you KNOW she's doing willingly (i.e. kissing, hugging, sex, talking, dancing, hanging out....anything!). If you ever have doubts about a woman being comfortable doing something, then STOP immediately. And don't start again until you know that's what she wants. There are so many women in the world, you never have to force anything. Just find someone that wants what you want, so that you both can enjoy it together.

3. ***Don't forget that relationships are only in part about you.*** Sex makes children. Having children is about raising them to be healthy and productive. You also belong to a community. It might not feel like it sometimes, if you haven't had a lot of people looking out for you. But you're at least a part of the Black community. And we have a responsibility to show the world examples of excellence, since we were the first humans here. You also might be a part of a religious community, or live in a neighborhood, and one of the best ways to make any community better is by building and maintaining healthy families.

   Good relationships are connected by the spirit AND the science of evolution. The human design requires us to come together.

You wouldn't be here reading this right now if it weren't for God/Nature, and the relationship (however long it lasted) between the two people that made you. So the next generation depends on you.

4. **Never abandon the people you're responsible for.** Don't abandon your family. They're probably not perfect, but you have to stick together anyway. And when you make a family then yall have to do whatever yall can to stick together. When you make children, take care of them. No matter what! Even if it's difficult. Even if you stop liking the mother. Even if your money's tight. Do whatever you can to spend time with your children. The relationship between a father and his child is

5. one of the most important connections on the planet.

   Don't let anyone trick you into thinking that women are your enemy. When I listen to some men talk it seems like they hate women. Those men have fallen for the worst trick played on Black people: turning Black men against our own women. Women have supported us, and maintained the health of our families, through some of the most difficult situations you can imagine. When most Black men understand that and start building healthy partnerships with Black women, then there is nothing we cannot accomplish.

6. **Ask an older man you respect to add a few more to this list.**

   _____

   _____

   _____

CHAPTER 4
MANHOOD

*I can save you some time. You can avoid reading any more if your eyes are tired, or if you'd rather go watch TV. This chapter isn't for every male. We are all born with the potential to be great, but we can also choose NOT to be. You might be one of those people. You may have already decided NOT to contribute anything to the world. You might be happy living and dying as someone else's puppet. **If that's you** then you should probably just put this book down and go play video games. There are people making lots of money off of prisons, cemeteries and war. They need you. They have spots waiting for you... **If that is NOT you,** if you actually want life to mean something then this chapter was written for YOU.*

Wearing a white coat and a stethoscope around your neck don't make you no doctor. Putting on a hard yellow hat and tool belt don't make you a construction worker. Making a baby don't make you a father. And carrying a gun doesn't make you a soldier. **Just because you wear a man costume, doesn't mean you are a real man**. Even if you really look like one. Your broad shoulders won't do it. A beard and a moustache won't trick me. Being mature doesn't have anything to do with what you look like. <u>Being a man is more than appearance</u>.

What Does It Mean to Be a Man?

I don't know <u>when</u> I became I man. There was no announcement or ceremony. No certificate. I had ceremonies AND certificates to let me know when I finished enough school. But **nothing happened when I graduated from a boy into a man**.

At what point do you think a boy should be considered a man? Puberty? When he's 16 and can drive? Eighteen and can vote or die in war? Twenty-one and can drink? (Who even came up with those random ages?) Does a boy become a man after he gets a girl pregnant? Or graduates from college? Lives on his own? Buys his mom a house? Serves jail time? Kills another man? Saves another man's life?

We need some manhood guidelines. We need standards. Lots of males are claiming to be men, because they can define it however they want. But their thoughts and actions are still on the level of a ten-year-old boy—playing games, being lazy, bragging, lying, and not being responsible for anything.

When I think about all the problems in Black communities, it seems like most of them could be solved by the presence of more men. For example, fatherless parenting, children being uneducated or miseducated by schools that are designed for them to fail, police brutality, ignorant media, legal and illegal drug dealers, limited access to healthcare, violence against women, self-hatred, poverty, etc. **If more men stepped up, and worked together with women, we could fix all of these problems**. Our efforts could be even stronger if we worked together with other communities of color, across different religions, and with queer and transgendered communities. Our personal preferences should not keep us from fighting together to improve a world we all share whether we like it or not.

I'm not the expert on manhood. I don't think there can be such a thing. Each person is different, and what it means to be a man will change depending on your age and the needs of your community. However, I do have a few ideas to consider towards our evolving definition of manhood. I share these standards of manhood to begin the conversation that I hope you continue by reading others' ideas, watching documentaries, and talking to your brothers, friends and elder men about manhood.

Standards of Manhood

The rest of the chapter talks about standards that all of us should be able to demonstrate, once you have become a man:
1. Define yourself.
2. Actively figure out your purpose.
3. Learn to use your emotions.
4. Be consistent.
5. Be flexible.

6. Take responsibility.
7. Don't pretend to have power. Create and cultivate real power.
8. Have vision.
9. Don't forget that women are under attack, too.
10. Think! Think! Think!
11. Be Happy. Smile. Laugh. Enjoy life!
12. Serve something greater than yourself.

Man Standard #1: Define yourself

Imagine an alien from outer space wants to come to the United States to find out who Black men are. It will start by looking through magazines with "BLACK MEN" in the title. As the alien flips through the pages it will see mostly rims, naked women, and shoe advertisements. Next, the alien will listen to music on the radio or watch rap videos. It will think Black men just like to party, drink, smoke weed, collect women and buy jewelry. Then maybe the alien will watch Black men in the movies and think we're all violent gangbangers. Next the alien will watch the news and think Black men are criminals. Finally, the alien will go to schools and read the history books, and conclude that there were only a few Black men, ever, who gave anything important to the world.

A lot of people think Black men are dumb, athletic and scary. A lot of people only know what they see on TV and hear in the music.

But in real life, if you sit down and ask Black men, "What are the things in life that are **most important** to you?" most of us wouldn't say anything about cars, violence, jewelry or parties. Most men will say the <u>most</u> important things in their life are family, friends, their children, or God. Which should make you wonder, why don't those things show up more in the TV shows, music, or movies about us?

We need to control how we define ourselves. That's too much power to give away. It's scary thinking about how much of our self-definition comes from the Europeans who enslaved us. For example, most Black people's names (Washington, Smith, Johnson, Green, Wilson, Robinson, McDonald, Jones, Thompson... Cartman) come directly from the White people who thought they owned us. So did the English language you're reading right now. And the names of the days and months. Just about everything I use to understand who, where, and when I am in the world comes through White people. Which doesn't necessarily mean there's anything wrong with Whiteness. Their culture just cannot help us figure out for ourselves who we are.

> *"I am America. I am the part you won't recognize. But get used to me. Black, confident, cocky; my name, not yours; my religion, not yours; my goals, my own; get used to me."*
> —Muhammad Ali

So <u>who are we</u>? Who are Black men? Or should I say African-American men? Is that a label we still want? On the one hand, **America** hasn't been that kind to us. But at the same time, we were visiting this land before Europeans. Then after Europeans started capturing us and bringing us here in chains, we spent hundreds of years working the land, building American roads, cities and its economy. We literally built this country. I think we've earned a right to be here.

What about the 'African' in the <u>African</u>-American label, should we keep that? A lot of Black people don't want to be connected to Africa because we believe the lies we see on TV about Africa being full of war, poor hungry people, and AIDS. Some people still think all Africans walk around barefoot and live in trees. If that's you, then take a moment to search the internet for pictures of cities in Africa, like Lagos (Nigeria), Kinshasa (Congo), Abidjan (Ivory Coast), Nairobi (Kenya), Dakar (Senegal), Kampala (Uganda)… just to get started.

The simplest reason why it makes sense to keep 'African' in our definition is because that's where we come from. If someone kidnapped you today and took you to China, that wouldn't turn you into a Chinese person. You'd probably still call yourself an African American living in China. We are originally from Africa, and that will always be true, wherever we end up in the world.

Keeping the 'African' in <u>African</u>-American also has to be more about location. Defining who we are as Black men is about culture. How we dress, our religions, language, food, what we do for fun, our art, what we think about family, and our values. Without even trying, there's still a lot in our Black U.S. culture that has lasted from when we lived in Africa, before slavery. For example, our strong connections to family have always been a part of African culture. Our deep spirituality. Our ability to adapt. You also find African culture in current African-American lifestyle. For example, the drums and wordplay in hip-hop. The improvisation in jazz. The call/response or the spirit possession in church. Finally, we still have the same melanin in our blood that Africans all over the world have. That's what makes our skin darker. It also has special powers according to the book **Why Darkness Matters: The Power of Melanin in the Brain.**[1]

So far we've been discussing the question "Who are we?" as a GROUP of Black men in this country. But answering the question "Who am I?" as an INDIVIDUAL is slightly different. We might decide, as a group, that we like the labels 'African' or 'American', but as an individual I still have to deal with the fact that **country and continent names aren't real**. They are names someone made up to describe lines on a map that don't really exist. I can decide as an individual that *'I am African'*, but what does that really mean? I can say that 'I am *Obari'*, but that's just a name my parents found in a book. My name could've been Robert, Mustafa, or Toothpaste. Names don't really tell you who you are. I could say *"I am a psychologist"* or *"I am an artist"*. But what if I lose my job? Or decide to do something else? Am I defined by what I do?

After I take away all the <u>labels</u> I use to define myself, once I realize most of them are only partly real, then what am I left with? WHO AM I? And why am I here?

Man Standard #2:
Actively figure out your purpose.

> *"Don't ask what the world needs. Ask what makes you come alive, and go do it. Because what the world needs is people who have come alive."*

—Howard Thurman

You are alive for a reason. There is some thing, probably several things that you were created to do. We all have limited time on this earth in this body. We choose, every day, whether to waste that time, or to make the best of it. It's pretty easy to figure out which one you're doing. Just think about how you spend your day. What do you do with your moments? Are most of your hours in the day spent in school? And if so, are you really learning? Maybe you spend most of your hours working at a job. If so, does it serve <u>your</u> purpose or someone else's? Or do you spend most of your hours just chillin', watching TV, listening to music, playing on the internet, getting high, scrolling and texting?

Too many men wait until they're old to start looking back on their life and wonder if it had any <u>purpose</u>. Or they get shot, or get in a car accident, look death in the eye, then start to think about how to make their life mean something. **Don't wait!** Don't be sitting at somebody else's funeral and for the first time wonder if it would matter if you die. Think about it now! Do it every day. Any moment when you find yourself just coasting, existing, going through the motions, doing the same ol' same ol', you have to **stop**. Ask if there is a purpose to how you spend your time. If not, do something different. You must make an effort every day to live your purpose.

But how do I figure out what my purpose is?

The first step and the second step can be switched. You can start with either. It's up to you. Just pick the one you like better.

Step 1: Go inside yourself

> *I just needed time alone, with my own thoughts. Got treasures in my mind but couldn't open up my own vault.*
> —Kanye West[2]

What? Go inside myself? That sounds weird. What does that mean? This step towards finding your purpose happens all alone. Figure out some time, between 20 minutes and 2 hours, where you can sit in a silent room. With no distractions. No TV, turn off your phone, no music (unless you wanna start off with something like instrumentals or jazz, something without words). If you can't find a quiet room alone inside your home, workplace, school, or library, then go outside and walk. Or sit in a park. Or take a ride on the bus. Go somewhere where you won't see people you know. The point is that you want to spend some time just being alone, with no one but yourself.

While you're sitting alone in the quiet, try to <u>stop thinking</u>. Turn your brain on silent. Even when everything else is quiet, your brain is still gonna wanna keep working. Give it some time to shut down. Don't get frustrated. This part is not easy. Thoughts will keep trying to sneak into your head. The brain is kind of an asshole. The more you tell it to stop thinking, the more it will want to keep thinking. So don't force it. Just relax. When thoughts pop up, just ignore them. Let 'em float away like a cloud disappearing into the sky.

It may help to find something to focus on. For example, try to give all your attention to your **breathing**. (Works best with your eyes closed.) Think about the air surrounding you like a giant pool of water and you're sitting right in the middle. When you breathe in, imagine this air slowly being pulled into your nose (keep your mouth closed). Try pretending like the air changes colors as it enters your nose, like blue smoke. Going slowly into your nose, into the back of your throat, passing through the middle of your chest, filling up your lungs. Keep your chest still, while your stomach slowly fills like a balloon. Then, after your air balloon is full, hold it for three seconds. Then release the air, slowly out of your mouth. Keep your lips tight, so you can hear the air releasing like a tire. Picture the blue smoke leaving your mouth and floating back into the air, until your lungs are so empty that you can squeeze your stomach tight.

Keep focusing on that process over and over. Slowly breathing in and out. When new thoughts pop up, just ignore them, and go right back to focusing on your lungs filling up, and then emptying. The point of all this is to relax, especially your brain. You want to get your mind as clear as possible. Like a blank sheet of paper. Waiting for something to be written on it.

After you get your mind as clear as possible, you're ready to start receiving messages about your purpose. This part is like a conversation between you and God, or the Universe, or your Ancestors, or your Intuition. You simply ask the question: **"Why am I here?"** And wait for the answer. But it won't happen like on TV. You might not hear a deep loud voice coming from the sky. The answer is more likely to come in the form of visions. You will see images of yourself doing the things you're supposed to do. You will see your ideal self, the best possible version of you. And you can sit there, watching these visions of you like a movie, floating through your mind.

Most of the time, the visions you get about your **purpose** won't be brand new. They shouldn't be that much of a surprise to you. It'll be something someone said to you before. Or something you've already thought about. It might be something you're already doing, so the quiet moments will just confirm that you're already on the right path.

Step 2: Go outside yourself

Your purpose is partly informed by the people around you. "Informed" means that while you're figuring out your **purpose** other people should have *input*, or give guidance. (But you don't want anyone else telling you exactly what your purpose is.)

Sometimes our friends and family will notice things about us that we don't see. Pay attention to that. If you always hearing people say *"you're really good at…" or "you would be a perfect…"*, then maybe there's something to it. Even if you don't believe them at first.

The goal of this <u>purpose finding</u> step is to be **active!** Do stuff. Go places. Try new things. Look for organizations to volunteer with or join. Start with your natural talents and interests. If you like music, then find a program that promotes positive music in the community, and offer your skills. If you like dance, find kids to teach dance to. If you like reading, set aside a couple of hours a week to tutor. You can go to any mosque, church, community center, etc. and they will have programs you can join. If you're a student, your school also has lots of clubs and organizations.

If you can't find anything to join, then create it. Unfortunately, the world has plenty of problems to solve. So if you see a problem in your community, then come up with an idea to solve it. Ask your friends to help you. It could be as simple as picking up the trash on the street. Or more complicated, like organizing a radio boycott, starting a community garden, or demanding your mayor spend more tax money on the youth.

Just do something! Anything. It doesn't have to have a clear plan. **As you do it, you will get a better idea of whether it fits your purpose.** Pay attention to which activities feel better to you. Think about what <u>parts</u> of the activities you enjoy. For example, it could be the teaching, or interacting with people, planning, problem solving, working with your hands, making people laugh, serving, researching, motivating people, etc. Some things will come easy to you. Some will be challenging, in a good way. Others will make you feel like "that's not really my thing". As you're working, there's a couple of questions you should always ask yourself:

- Is this helping anyone?
- Am I gaining any skills?
- Would I keep doing this for free or should I try to figure out how to make money doing it?
- Does this feel like what I was born to do?

Step 3: Repeat first two steps over and over again

Just keep doing them back and forth. Do one *(go inside)*, then the other *(go outside).* Then do the first one again. This way, you will never get stuck. You will stay involved in action that benefits the world, while also taking breaks, for yourself, to make sure you're on track. Work, work, work. Stop. Rest. Check in. Work. Check in. Rest. Work, work. Check in. Work. Rest, rest, rest. Check in. Work... and keep repeating. Until the world is fixed.

Man Standard #3:
The secret to making a billion dollars in two years!

"If you are silent about your pain, they'll kill you and say you enjoyed it."
—Zora Neale Hurston

Men be trying to act like we don't feel shit. We pretend like women are the only ones with emotions. But that's a lie. I know men get sad. And men get scared. We just don't like to admit it. Plus, we're taught to never show it (unless it's through sports). Which might not change soon. But *what _does_ need to change*, is **we** have to be more honest **with ourselves** about how we feel. Because showing anger, when you're really scared, can get you killed. And being sad, but staying high so you don't feel it, can also kill you.

There is a lot of power in your emotions. You just have to learn to understand them, and use them right.[3] Black men are taught to avoid emotions. We are told feelings are weak. But it's a trick, which actually **makes you** weaker. Emotions are **signals** that tell you there's something important you need to pay attention to. They're like an alarm (Wake up! Emergency!) saying there's something in your life, or something in your mind, that needs to change.

If you always ignore the emotional signals, then you will never make the necessary changes. And that's how Black men get stuck. We'll have plans, things we want to accomplish, relationships we want to be successful, career goals, etc. And we get frustrated when we can't move as fast or far as we want. One key to your success is to **stop avoiding** your feelings.

How do men usually avoid feeling? Pain hurts. So men have lots of ways we escape. To not feel. Some men get obsessed with making or spending **money**. Some men work extra hard to **seem tough**, to thug their feelings out of them. I used to use women. Not sex so much, just the attention and affection of women. **Alcohol and weed** are probably the most popular things Black men use to avoid feeling. They are designed to numb your emotions.

Weed and alcohol are like the stuff doctors and dentists give before surgery (anesthesia), so the patient doesn't feel anything. Imagine for a moment, you are training a young boxer. You want him to be the best fighter in the world, so yall jog, lift weights, work on his hooks, uppercuts, and footwork. But you don't want him to get hurt. So you give him medicine to numb his body while he trains. This way, he can get jabbed in the jaw 20 times and never feel any pain. *But he needs to feel the pain.* You are crippling him by numbing him, not helping him. Getting hit and feeling pain is the best way he'll learn to move faster or defend himself. When it's time for the real fight he won't be ready. Just like a lot of men who use **weed** and **alcohol** to numb their emotions. The next time you see a guy getting drunk or high, you should think *"I wonder if he's trying to not feel right now."* And if he's your friend, maybe you should ask him.

Okay, so I won't avoid my emotions anymore. Now what am I supposed to do with them? Some emotions are like the green light on a traffic signal. When you feel **happy, excited**, or **peaceful**, that means GO. Keep doing whatever you were doing. And enjoy the feeling.

Emotions like **fear, sadness** and **anger** are like a yellow light. SLOW DOWN. Figure out what needs to change. You might even want to STOP. Especially if something gets you so angry that you feel like you might lose control. Don't just keep going, business as usual, like everything's okay. Sometimes, though, your actions will have to keep moving on. You will still have to go to work and school, and still have to take care of your kids. But even then, your brain should slow down, and pay closer attention to how you're feeling and what might need to change.

A lot of times our bodies know what we feel before our minds do. Everybody's body works differently, but there are several areas you should pay attention to. Your temperature. If you start to feel warm, it might mean you're <u>nervous</u> or <u>angry</u> about something. And your **heartbeat** might get faster if you're <u>nervous</u> or <u>excited</u>. Your whole body might respond to <u>sadness</u>— you'll have **low energy** and feel slow, like you're carrying extra weight.

For me, my **stomach** is the place I feel a lot of my emotions. I can be in the middle of a normal conversation, everything is fine, then I'll feel a quick, sharp, tight pain in the middle of my stomach. Then in my mind I say, *"Hmm, that's interesting; something doesn't feel right. Am I nervous? I wonder why..."* And since my stomach is such an important place for my emotional signals, I have to be careful what I put in there. If I fill it up with crappy food and drink, then I won't get as clear a signal. That's why people fast (like Ramadan or Lent) when they want extra clarity. Your diet, physical health and emotional health are all connected.

Which emotions should I pay closest attention to? There are many emotions that we experience throughout our lives. I'll talk about three in this section you should pay particular attention to: sadness, fear and anger.

1. SADNESS.

Sad is the most common human emotion. Life can be really shitty. We have all types of disappointments and loss. Black men get sad a lot, but almost never talk about it. If you think you're the only Black man that gets sad, trust me, you're not. I'm a psychologist, so men tell me things they normally wouldn't tell other people.

You have had a reason to be sad if you have ever:
• Lost a friend or family member • Witnessed violence • Needed more money than you had • Been misunderstood • Had a hard time finding or keeping a job • Served time • Got embarrassed in front of people • Been lied to or lied about • Been physically, verbally or sexually abused • Loved someone that didn't love you back • Been to a funeral • Worked hard for a goal you didn't reach • Experienced racism…

There are levels of sadness. A small disappointment can put you in a bad mood for an hour, until you forget about it and move on. A major loss or several tragedies in a row can make you think about killing yourself. **If you ever think about killing yourself, please, go tell someone you need help immediately.** And if they don't help, please, <u>go tell someone else</u>. Suicide is a decision you can only make once. And it's the wrong decision, every time. "Suicide doesn't end the pain. It just passes it on to someone else." (-*Kim Kirkup).* There is <u>always</u> something to live for. Even if it doesn't feel like it in the darkest moments.

How do you fix it? When you're sad, there's a couple of things you can do. **Talk about it** with someone you trust, to get it off your chest. Or express it through ***music***, or ***drawing***. If you don't want to talk, you can still get it out by ***writing*** down how you feel, and why. It's good to keep a notebook or journal around. (The best part is looking back at stuff you wrote and seeing how much you've changed.) The easiest way to release sadness is to **cry**. You don't have to tell nobody about it. No one has to see you. It can happen all alone, in a closet. I do my best crying driving in the car by myself.

Sadness over time is like a cancer. It works by tricking you into thinking you're not valuable. It tells you it's not worth trying to do <u>anything</u>. So you have to fight sadness, real hard, by reminding yourself as often as you can, that **you are important**, smart, talented, capable and all the things you love about yourself. This is not the time to be humble. Then <u>you have to force yourself to stay active</u>. You won't feel like doing anything, because that's what sadness does, but you gotta get up and get out anyway. Exercise. Go visit friends and family. Make yourself do the things you love doing, until they feel fun again.

Be careful not to do things while trying to make yourself feel better <u>that will cause even more pain later</u>. That's like having a sore throat and taking medicine with heart attacks as a side effect. For example, if shopping makes you feel better, but you spend money you ain't got, then later you might lose your car or house. Then you'll really be sad. Drugs, alcohol and sex can also give temporary relief from sadness, **but cause even worse problems later on**.

Pay very close attention to **your thoughts** while you feel sad. It's best to catch your thoughts <u>right at the first moment</u> you notice the sad feeling. That'll help you figure out why you're sad.

And you will see if you have any thoughts in your brain that are causing more problems. Sometimes we have leftover thoughts in our brain that other people stuck in there. <u>We forget they're not ours</u>. For example, your parents, aunt, uncle or a teacher might've told you that you were stupid or ugly when you were a kid. Later you realized that's **not true**, but when you get sad, their voice might sneak back up into your brain.

So at that moment, when you feel sad, if you catch yourself thinking *"I am a fuck up"* or *"I am a mistake"*, then you have to replace that **false** thought with a **true** thought: *"I messed up that time"* or *"I made a mistake."* Another example: you're sad, maybe feel like you are about to cry, and you catch the though in your head *"The world is unfair and I'm cursed."* You have to ignore that (because it's too broad to be true), shake it out of your brain, and replace it with something <u>specific</u> like, *"I don't understand why my parents left me, and I miss them."* Take control of your brain. It's in <u>your</u> head. So use it for your own good.

The absolute best medicine for sadness is **gratitude**. If you lost something or someone, tell your brain to focus on the people and things you <u>still have</u>. Be thankful. If you're still breathing, and healthy, and have food to eat, and a place to sleep, then there's something to appreciate. Even if it's just hope for the future, there's always, always a reason to be thankful.

2. FEAR.

Men don't like to admit being **afraid**. We think it means you're weak. Nobody wants to feel like a punk. When you feel fear, there's usually some type of threat or danger. Like if you're alone and see a gang of police come at you. Or if a judge is deciding how much time to give you. Or if you get a call that someone you love was in a car accident.

Anybody who says *"I ain't afraid of nothing!"* is afraid of being honest. Fear covers a lot of ground. You can be afraid of **change**. Of **growing up**. You can have secrets you're afraid of being exposed. You can be afraid of being vulnerable in relationships. You can be afraid of rejection. Or loneliness.

How do you fix it? The most important thing to help with fear is **support**. If you're afraid of a danger, then you need to protect yourself somehow. Protection and support can come in a lot of different ways:

- If you are at home, you and your kids are sleep and somebody breaks in with a weapon, at that moment having a registered gun might make you feel safer.
- If you are afraid something in your life might not work out, then you may ask for support from the spiritual world. You can call on your ancestors, Orisha, Jesus, or pray for Allah or God's support.
- If you are afraid of quitting your job and starting your own business, you can find a mentor, someone else that's already done it, or start a business with a group of people who are putting their resources together.
- If you are afraid of being vulnerable with your girlfriend, you might ask her for support by saying *"I have something really difficult to tell you, and I'm afraid you might not like me as much. But can you please try to be open-minded and remember that I love you?"*

3. ANGER.

Black men are really good at showing **anger**. Especially towards other Black people. We're so comfortable with anger that we show anger at times when we really feel <u>sad</u> or <u>scared</u>. Which is a big problem.

Anger is a feeling caused by being **violated** or **disrespected** in some way. Anger is a natural response to being insulted, offended, lied to, lied about, threatened, attacked, or abused. Some of the same things that make you <u>sad</u> can also make you <u>angry</u>. (I usually feel the anger first, and sadness will come later.)

> *"Anger is like a fire. If we contain fire appropriately and allow it to burn safely, it nourishes us, keeps us alive, and provides us with warmth and light. If we let it rage out of control, it damages or destroys us. If we suffocate it and stamp it out, eventually the cold and the dark seep in our bones, and we become numb."*
> —Harville Hendrix[4]

I get more worried these days when I meet Black men that aren't angry. We have so many of our brothers getting locked up in prisons, or not being able to get decent work after they served their time. Then there's the unemployment. The innocent people being shot. Plus, the schools are so quick to medicate, punish or get rid of gifted Black men they don't understand. And there's the garbage being put out on the radio in the name of hip-hop. And a court system that sometimes makes it hard for us to raise our own children. There's tons of reasons for Black men to be mad! But <u>what do we do</u> with all this anger?

How do you fix it? When something violates or disrespects you, there's two responses you can have: go towards it or go away from it. In other words, <u>confront</u> it or <u>distance</u> yourself from it. For example, you might think America is violating Black men, and you are angry about it. So you can either go towards it—organize, create alternative institutions, protest, boycott, march, run for office, or somehow become politically active to confront the government. Or *go away from it*—you can leave, move to another country. Another example: you found out your girlfriend has been lying to you about something and you are really upset about it. You can go to her, tell her you caught her lying, tell her how upset you are, and ask her to explain herself and/or apologize. Or you can break up with her.

Too often, men are angry at one thing, but take it out on someone else. Or they just complain about it, and don't ever do nothing about it. If you never recognize the source of your anger, then you will always be angry. A lot of Black people are mad at White people, but only show anger, hostility, and violence towards <u>each other</u>. White people never even realize we're mad. They just watch the news and wonder why we keep fighting and killing each other.

Sometimes men get drunk with anger. They'll be so mad that they lose control of their words and actions. When you feel that violated or disrespected, you need **space** and **time** to calm down. The yelling, screaming, punching and throwing things, tells the people around you: get back, stay away, I need space. But now here's where it gets tricky. If you need ***space* when you're angry**, but you need ***support* when you're afraid**, then what happens when men are only taught to show anger, even if they <u>really feel</u> sad or afraid? If anger is the only thing we show, then we never get what we need if we're sad or afraid. In fact, it's even worse than that. We get **the opposite** of what we need: <u>distance</u> instead of <u>support</u>.

> *This section really wasn't about making a billion dollars in two years. I was afraid you wouldn't read it if I said it was about "feelings". My bad for lying. The real title for this manhood standard is:* ***Learn to use your emotions.***

Man Standard #4 : Be consistent

You know "that guy" who's always changing his positions? If he's with one group of friends, he loves New York (for example), it's his favorite city in the world. Then with another group of friends he thinks NY is hyped up, too crowded and dirty. That guy is a people pleaser. Always going with the crowd. He will say or do whatever he thinks people will like. **You don't wanna be that guy.**

If you don't like a song, you just don't like a song. Don't let people change your mind by calling you a 'hater'. Stand your ground. Defend your arguments. You have a right to your opinions. Establish the kind of reputation where everyone might not agree with you all the time, or like you every day, <u>but they will respect you</u> for being genuine, confident and consistent.

Man Standard #5: Be flexible.

Yes, I know this is very different from the last thing I just said. Which just means you have to pay attention to **when** it makes more sense to be consistent OR be flexible. Sometimes you gotta stick to your guns. Other times you should wonder if bringing guns might make the situation worse.

We live in a complicated and changing world. Sometimes we try to make things too simple. We live by rules that are too strict. For example:

1. Don't start nothing you can't finish! *(But what if you realize, right in the middle of it, that it was a really stupid idea?)*
2. Never say never! *("when you say never say never, you done said never twice"—Mos Def)*
3. Don't snitch! *(unless you got information that can keep another innocent victim from being hurt, raped or killed)*

Being flexible also means NOT just being good at one thing. **You want to have several sets of skills** (which can mean several sources of income). I understand that sometimes you gotta focus all your attention on the one thing you're most passionate about. But don't spend too much time on it. If you're 42 and your rap career ain't jumped off yet, then it's probably not gonna happen.

Whatever your thing is—it could be rapping, basketball or school—you don't want to spend all your time and energy doing it. Even if you're amazing at it! You want to have a couple of tricks up your sleeve. Because there's only a couple of spots on the radio, the NBA, and in graduate school. **If you love hip-hop**, while you're working on your rhymes and performance— also learn about the business side, management, public relations, advertising, fashion, production, blogging, magazines, engineering, film, etc. **If you love basketball**, while you're working on your jump shot—also learn about physical therapy, being a sports analyst and announcer, sports law, coaching, shoe and apparel design, video game production, and stadium/team ownership. **If you love school**, while you're completing all their assignments—also learn about information not included in the curriculum, and how to incorporate the arts, and how to give the stuff you learn back to people with less access, and always stay involved in community service and extracurricular activities to make your resume more competitive and your life more dynamic.

Man Standard #6: Take responsibility.

"Even though I'm not guilty of the charges they gave me, I'm not innocent in terms of the way I was acting. I'm just as guilty for not doing things. Not with this case but with my life. I had a job to do and I never showed up. I was so scared of this responsibility that I was running away from it."

—Tupac (written while in prison) [5]

It's hard being responsible for others. Especially when you feel like no one has been responsible for you. You might think your parents, family, or community let you down. And here I am, asking you to step up, be leaders, and fix all of Black people's problems. Meanwhile you still might be struggling to take care of yourself. **Even if that's true**, the world would be a much better place if all the men, _at the very least_, **took responsibility for the children they make**. Being a provider isn't just about money. Time, skills, and attention can be even more important for your children.

Also, don't get used to blaming everybody else for your problems. You can blame others for part of it, but **never all of it**. For example, White people have done terrible things to Black people. But, at the same time, it's not _their_ fault you don't work harder or smarter. There's no White person coming into your room putting unhealthy food in your mouth or forcing you to watch TV. It's **not** your fault you were born into a world with so many problems and so much unfairness. However, it is still your responsibility to do what you can to make it better.

You should always start with yourself though. Start by being responsible for what you say and do. Figure out what things are important to you. Then prioritize them. If something or someone is a priority in your life, then **your time will show that**. You are responsible for how you spend your time. So if you say family is the most important thing to you, then when you look back at your day/week/years, most of your time should've been spent with or for your family.

Man Standard #7: Don't pretend to have power. Create and cultivate real power.

Black men in the U.S. have gotten really good at copying White men. We see the power they get from resources they steal. We watch them use threats and violence all over the world to gain power. Then we try to make ourselves feel powerful by doing the same. We waste a lot of energy (and money) learning how to look, sound and act like we in charge.

According to Dr. Amos Wilson, *"No Black person has ever been taught to think like 'White folks'. If you thought like Whites, you would want your own nations, to control your own neighborhoods, to control your own economy, to have your own military, to control the resources in your ground. Blacks come out of these schools and universities to be highly educated servants, slaves not in control of their own destiny."* [6]

Real power would mean Black people could provide our most basic needs amongst ourselves. Food, land, transportation, electricity, gas, technology, and education. But right now, we go outside ourselves, to other races, for all those things. Real power would mean Black children go to schools where they learn Black history all year, not just in one month. Real power would mean we'd print money with the faces of our ancestors on it. Real power, at the least, means that we could vote for leaders and politicians that respond to the specific needs of the Black community.

But we settle for **fake power**. Black men are satisfied if their gang controls a few blocks (that actually belong to the city). Or if we have a good enough job to buy a nice car, wear fancy suits, and pay our mortgage. Or we hope to be famous entertainers and athletes (who still answer to a White boss). Or we get feelings of fake power from **bullying**. <u>Those are the weakest Black men</u>. A bully makes fun of people with mental or physical disabilities. A bully uses his strength to threaten or intimidate people that act different, have less money, are smaller or younger. A bully uses violence against women and children.

Another group that gets bullied a lot is gay people. Gay men make some straight men uncomfortable. Maybe they think they're gonna turn them gay? Regardless of your religious or personal belief about gayness, there is no excuse to make fun of them, bully them, or try to harm them because they're different from you. One of the toughest Black men in U.S. history, the founder of the Black Panther Party had this to say about homosexuals:

> "Whatever your personal opinions and your insecurities about homosexuality and the various liberation movements among homosexuals and women (and I speak of the homosexuals and women as oppressed groups), we should try to unite with them in a revolutionary fashion."
> —Huey P. Newton[7]

Real power needs to be developed **internally** and **externally**. <u>Internally</u> means on the inside, within one's self. <u>Externally</u> means outside of yourself, in the world, as a group. (And **cultivate**, from the title of this section, means to work on something consistently, so it builds and grows over time). Real **internal power** uses what we learn about our individual purpose to create power and meaningful lives. It requires self-knowledge, discipline and patience. With real internal power you can go anywhere in the world and no matter what's happening around you, you can feel freedom. And you can also use your internal power to achieve **success** in as many ways as you can imagine it.

External power happens on the outside. It's the kind of power that leaves a mark. It happens best when powerful individuals join together to make powerful couples, powerful families, and powerful groups. Black people have to figure out ways to work together, to support each other. We need to organize ourselves, and build institutions that last. We need to fight and destroy systems of White supremacy (which is the false idea that White people's culture, values, styles, and intelligence is better than all the other peoples' in the world). And the goal isn't to replace them with systems of Black supremacy, but to create a world where everyone can benefit. The planet itself won't survive much longer under the myth of White supremacy. Global warming, pollution, and whole species of animals disappearing, should remind us of that.

Black people have won **everything** we came together to fight for. We won our freedom from slavery, we stopped lynchings, we've created our own schools and gained access to the best White schools. We won the right to vote and elected a Black president. We're on TV, radio, writing books, inventing technology, running companies. Whenever Black people decide we want to accomplish anything, history shows us that we can do it. Especially when we join together with other groups of color like Latinos or Native Americans, and <u>anyone</u> <u>else</u> who is serious about justice and freedom for Black people, people of color, oppressed people, poor people, and children.

So what will we fight for now? How should we use our power? To abolish the prison system? To create a new nation? To travel to outer space? To protect the natural resources (oil, diamonds, land) of Africa? To create a new religion or language? <u>We can do anything we want</u>. All we have to do is decide to do it together.

> If you want to go fast, go alone. If you want to go far, go together.
> —African proverb

Man Standard #8: Have vision.

Imagine a clear plastic bag, full of tiny puzzle pieces. Someone hands it to you and asks you to put the pieces together. You spread all the pieces on a table, and start trying to connect the pieces. But then you might ask, **"What is the final picture supposed to look like?"** Normally, when you buy a puzzle from the store, it comes in a box with the final picture on the front of the box. So you know what you're creating. It is very difficult to put puzzles together, solve problems, build anything, without a *vision* of what you want it to look like in the end.

You should have a <u>personal</u> <u>vision</u> for your life. And we should have a <u>collective</u> <u>vision</u> as a Black community for what life will look like after we win this fight.

Personal Vision

I used to want to be a doctor. I wanted to go to college and study medicine. When I was a teenager, I had a vision of myself as an adult, having a family and working somewhere as a doctor. Because my dad was a doctor. He was my vision for manhood growing up.

You used to be able to go into an elementary school and ask a bunch of boys what they wanted to be when they grew up and get a bunch of different answers: firefighter, musician, lawyer, mechanic, plumber, actor, etc. Because a lot of boys want to be like the adult men they see every day. These days, a lot of boys don't see their fathers and other men every day. So their visions of manhood are shaped more by TV. And when you see successful Black men on TV, they're usually rappers, athletes, or entertainers. So when you ask most boys these days what they want to be when they grow up, it's rappers, athletes, or entertainers.

Black men need to have more variety again in our visions for our personal future. If we don't have our fathers as good role models, then we should find teachers, or mentors somewhere else. We all need someone we admire so we can follow in their footsteps. Not to do exactly what they do, but to have a blueprint. It's really hard to <u>be</u> it - if you can't <u>see</u> it.

Collective Vision

Black people in the U.S. have been fighting for freedom since we were brought here enslaved. **But what does freedom**

look like? How do you know when you've got it? We're not fighting to end slavery anymore, or vote, or go to the same schools as White people. So what are we fighting for? **We have to figure out what our vision for freedom looks like now.**

If racism ended tomorrow, how would our lives, homes, and communities look? If White supremacy disappeared next week, and we lived in our own perfect Black land, with Black president, congress, judges, mayors, cops and teachers, in a country named…let's say Blacktopia… would we still even have a president, congress, judges, cops, etc.? What would Blacktopia smell like? What would we eat? How would we teach children or entertain ourselves? We need to be able to imagine a vision for what free Black people in 2050 will be doing after the struggle for freedom has been won. So that we can know <u>how</u> to fight for it and begin to create it right now.

Man Standard #9:
Don't forget that women are under attack, too.

I'm not talking about women in general. I'm talking about specific women. My little sisters. Our cousins. Your daughters. They are under attack too, by racism, sexism, the myth of White supremacy, poverty, miseducation, the prison system, police brutality, corporate hip-hop, and sexual abuse. Black men sometimes get so focused on our struggle that we forget that. We even get so confused sometimes we think we're fighting against Black women! We forget that women were on those torture ships coming from Africa, in chains right next to us. They were having our babies on those ships! And they've been having and raising our babies, including you, ever since. (Spoiler alert: They're probably gonna keep having them in the future too.)

"But what about the women that act like bitches and ho's?" is the next question I usually get from young men. This question is the main reason rap music gets away with such ugly lyrics. Women listen to it and be like ***"They ain't talking about me."*** And men listen thinking ***"They ain't talking about all women, definitely not my mama."*** The attacks against Black people in this country have wounded everybody. So if you meet a woman who is used to being disrespected, who may have never been loved genuinely, who may not know how brilliant and worthy she is, then you should not take advantage of that. She needs healing, support and care, just like the rest of us. It's a weak excuse to treat a woman wrong just because she lets you.

Man Standard #10: Think! Think! Think!

"Rarely do we find men who willingly engage in hard, solid thinking. There is an almost universal quest for easy answers and half-baked solutions. Nothing pains some people more than having to think."
—Martin Luther King

Always think. Wonder. Explore. Learn. Your brain is one of the most powerful tools on the planet, so use it! The people in charge have created a world designed to <u>keep you from thinking</u>. If you don't think, then you can't figure out how to gain any real power. That's why there are so many distractions. Twitter, Facebook, reality TV, iPads, texting, YouTube, Netflix, music videos, songs, magazines, etc. You could wake up in the morning scrolling social media, listen to music on your headphones all day, and fall asleep watching TV - never having your own original thought. A lot of schools are designed for the same purpose, to keep you from thinking. You spend all day being told what to know and following rules. Then you're rewarded during test time for showing how much information you could memorize. But that's still not thinking. Still not analyzing, and questioning, and solving problems, and figuring out ways to understand information from different perspectives.

The best tool for a critical thinker is a **question**. Anytime you hear or see something… ***anything***, think of questions you can ask about it:

Why did he say that? What else could he have said instead of that? How does he know that? What does it mean to know? Is "knowing" different from believing? Does someone benefit from me believing what he's saying? How does this make me feel? What if he's wrong? How would that affect me, or the world? Does any of this matter? Are these questions helping me? Am I overthinking this?

When someone asks **why** you said or did something, you don't want to always be like…. ***"Uh, I don't know."*** That means you didn't really think about it first. The more you think, the more you can live life on purpose. You want to do things for a reason. Too many people do stuff just because it feels good. Not because it also makes sense. ***"Because it feels good"*** is a bad reason to have sex, do drugs, or hit somebody. But it's also NOT a great reason to do stuff like vote, speak your mind, organize a rally, march or start a petition. Everything you do should be a part of a well thought out plan. You should think, in advance, about the desired, expected, and possible outcomes of all your actions.

Man Standard #11:
Be Happy! Smile. Laugh. Enjoy life!

Life should be fun! You are responsible for your own happiness. So make sure you're finding time to do stuff just because it makes you happy. Or just because it makes you laugh. As long as it does not cause suffering for someone else, then you should spend as much time as you can filling your life with as much joy as possible.

Black men don't talk enough about happiness. We always trying to be so hard. When was the time you giggled? And didn't look around to see if you got caught. We need to free ourselves up to be truly happy. To throw your head back and laugh till your stomach hurts. Sometimes my son makes me so happy I cry. We've replaced happy with high or with pleasure. Real happiness comes from living your purpose. It feels like your whole body is filled with electricity. Like light is shooting out from the center of your chest. It's those moments when you stop and realize everything right now is amazing and you submit to the perfect peace of it. That could happen while lying on a beach in Jamaica or sitting on a couch drinking lemonade watching Dave Chappelle. It's that happiness that makes all the fight, struggle, and sadness worth it.

Happiness is different for everybody, but you should still be able to measure your life joy by these three questions:
1. Do you have something valuable to do?
2. Do you have someone to love?
3. Do you have something to look forward to?[8]

If you have all these things, then cherish them. Help other people find their happiness. So it can spread like fire. If you don't have all three of those things, then go find them. Urgently, like your life depends on it.

Man Standard #12:
Serve something greater than yourself.

In this life, you will either be **used** or **useful**. I prefer to be useful. When I die, I want people to say "I'm glad he was here." I'd like to leave the Earth better than I found it. So I think often about being useful. Helping others. Fixing things. Making people's lives better. One of my favorite quotes is: "There is a wonderful mythical law of nature that the three things we crave most in life— happiness, freedom, and peace of mind—are always attained by giving them to someone else." So serving makes me happy. I think about serving others as my tax for oxygen.

Sometimes, though, I get too focused on what I want, and how I feel or what I think. And I have to snap out of it. To remind myself that **this is all so much bigger than me!** I'm only alive because of my parents, so I owe them. I'm happy and healthy because of lots of people who taught me and gave me their best. Black people have so many ancestors who have fought and died for us. We are here because of them, and we all owe them. So that's what I remember, to keep perspective, when I start thinking too much about my personal problems and wishes.

Religious people have this pretty easy. If you believe in Olodumare, God or Allah (same thing), then you were taught to serve the spiritual world because it created all the life on Earth. Most religions agree that the best way to serve God is by serving people. The rituals and rules are <u>less important</u> than making sure poor people are taken care of and oppressed people are free. **So, you should probably be doing that.** I don't really believe in hell, but it sounds pretty annoying.

If you don't believe in God, then you still belong to a family that's bigger than you. And a community. You also might have children one day. And your children might have children. So you have a responsibility to do whatever you can to make their world a better place to live in. Because that's how humans evolve. And Black people have been being human longer than anyone else. So where we go next, our next level of human evolution, is up to you.

CHAPTER 5
MY STORY

You can't teach what you don't know, and you can't lead where you won't go. —African proverb

"On the plane. About to land at home. This shit doesn't make any sense. Impulse to write. Thanks Y***. Mix of emotions. Mostly trying to keep from accessing emotions. Not sure where they'll go. What the fuck do you mean he drowned? That doesn't make any sense. He's invincible in the water. Did that cracker doctor friend of his kill my dad?!!!! Naw, that's crazy. (Or is it?) Landed in Chicago. This is going to suck. I don't know what's going to happen now. I'm scared. I'm scared for us. I'm scared for him. I can't stand to imagine how it happened. I know he went out like a muthafuckin soldier. My dad doesn't drown. He's invincible. 7:55am. Happy Halloween. The scariest day of the year. I have to be a man now. No more time for playing. I have to be a man now."

(10/31/2005. From my personal journal)

T he first step towards better family and community is knowledge of self. Becoming our best self requires long honest looks in the mirror—without judgment. We have to ask ourselves tough questions. We should think about how our actions have affected other people. That means looking at the stuff you're proud of and the stuff you wish to forget. It is difficult and lonely work. Can't nobody do it for you. But it's worth it, because **you're worth it.**

This last chapter is <u>my</u> journey into manhood. I can't ask you to think about your mistakes, successes, and lessons learned, without doing the same for myself. I offer my story as an example of some questions you could ask yourself. Even when the answers are ugly. Even when it's sad or embarrassing. I offer my story with the hopes that it may help you understand your own story a little better.

My Family

My father is one of the greatest men I've known. And my mother was one of the most beautiful, intelligent and talented women ever. They're both gone now. My father drowned in a lake soon after he turned 50. A few years later my mother's brain stopped working—they're calling it dementia. Mom's still alive as I'm writing this, kinda. I was 25 years old when Dad died. I still had a lot of man stuff (and life stuff) to figure out and wasn't sure how I was gonna do it without him. Thankfully, my parents gave me so much that I still give them the credit for all of my success. Everything I am—good, bad, ugly, and beautiful—is because of them.

My father had eight children by five different women. His father had 22 children, also from five different women. Both of them were highly respected, successful, generous and brilliant Black men. They will live forever through their children, grandchildren, and great-grandchildren. As I was growing up developing ideas about women and dating I struggled to respect my father's and grandfather's approach, because I was also watching the pain it caused my mother.

That is still a great dilemma for me. On one hand, my mother suffered so much sadness and stress because of my father's decisions. Sometimes I wanted to go back in time and take all that pain away from her. But on the other hand, that would mean undoing the relationships my father had with other women that produced three of my little sisters. And my sisters mean the world to me! I couldn't imagine my life without them.

I carry that struggle with me as I try to develop and maintain healthy relationships with women. I hear my father saying to me "God created men to be with multiple women", but then I see my mother crying. It takes active sorting, picking and choosing, to figure out which parts of my father's example as a husband and father are good for me to keep. And which ones I should throw away. I learned a lot through experience—meeting women, going on dates, being in relationships, living with women, and having a child with one.

I wish men were more open about our experiences with women, and not just bragging. We could learn a lot from each other by sharing honestly, without fear. So instead of wishing, I'll start the conversation...

Ladies Man

I <u>love</u> women. I just completely adore them. I love their voice and the way their hair smells. I love their laugh. Sometimes I'd rather be around women than eat. I love the way their skin feels, their walk, their styles. I love listening to women talk, and watching them dance. I've always been a big flirt, since I was a teenager. And "flirt" is a fun word to use, but over the years my obvious love for women has earned me other less cute labels: womanizer, dog, pimp, player, and of course… <u>ladies</u> <u>man</u>.

I didn't only make dumb mistakes while dating in my 20s and early 30s. I made some good decisions, too. Created some healthy relationships, was pretty honest (usually), and treated women with respect (almost always). Those good decisions happened when I took a moment to listen to my higher self. Sometimes I'd say to myself *"How would I want someone to treat me in this situation?"* Or even better, *"How would I want a man to treat my sisters right now?"* I also learned a lot about myself in those other moments, too, when I was less careful and did <u>not</u> stop to think.

Mistakes are great teachers. Some of my most important lessons with women have come from my mistakes. It's hard to admit when we mess up. Even harder to share it in public. But I'd rather you learn it from me than be out there practicing on my sisters and cousins.

Lying

"Women can't really handle the whole truth" was the biggest lie I used to tell myself while dating as a young man. I have lied about all types of stuff—where I was going, who I was with, what I've done in the past with another girl. I've lied about how I feel. I've lied about having good days on bad ones, and bad ones on good days. I've lied about my skills and abilities to impress a woman. One of the worst lies I've told is about visions and plans for a future with a woman. That's the ultimate set-up.

My first problem with lying was that I have a bad memory. I would forget who I told what, then get caught up in a lie. That's embarrassing. 'Cause then I'd start lying more to get out of the lie I got caught with. It turns out to be way too much work. Over the years I've learned that being honest is much easier.

More importantly, I learned at the root of my lying was the desire to control and manipulate women. I somehow decided that I was intelligent enough to create truth from my imagination and outsmart emotions. So if I gave just enough information I could set up situations where I could have everything I wanted. I could have one girl thinking she's the only one and other girls thinking we could have a future together. And I'm sitting in the middle of it like a criminal mastermind. But every time, no matter how hard I tried to balance all the pieces, they always came tumbling down on top of me.

Cheating

I have also cheated in relationships, usually because I was confused and lacked discipline. Few things are more dangerous than a confused man. One of the ways to demonstrate strength in manhood is to have **clarity**. A man should be clear about who he is, what he wants, and what his values and priorities are. Sometimes a man can be unsure about things, but even during those times he should be clear about that. Don't pretend to be clear when you're not. That was the mistake I often made in relationships. I thought I wanted to be with someone, or I thought I was ready to handle the responsibility of commitment, but I wasn't sure. Which wasn't the problem. The problem was bringing women into my life under the illusion of clarity and the false hope of security.

I have hurt women really bad by cheating on them. Looking into a woman's eyes after she knows you betrayed her trust is one of the worst feelings in the world. I remember the first time I cheated on my girlfriend. I was in college. I had promised myself I'd never make a woman feel like my father made my mother feel. I was wrong. It broke my heart hearing a woman say words to me that reminded me of things I heard my mother say.

The "funny" thing about cheating is that it usually happens when a guy really cares about a woman. I remember going through lots of trouble trying to hide the cheating because I knew if my girlfriend found out, she would be really hurt by it. At the time I thought I was doing her a favor. Since the cheating had already happened, telling her would've meant hurting her on purpose. But that's some coward shit. The truth is, it hurts a woman so much more to find out on her own or through someone else.

Women often wonder: *"Why didn't he just leave?"* But I didn't want to leave. I wanted to stay in the relationship. But at the same time I was curious about what another girl would feel like, and that's the confusion (and lack of discipline). The other part of it was **greed**. I wanted to have everything all at once — the comfort of a stable, loving relationship AND the adventure of dating and meeting new people. When I'm single I miss being in a relationship and when I'm in a relationship I miss being single. So cheating is a weak man's way of trying not to choose.

In the end, the consequences of cheating are never worth it. It feels terrible to hurt a woman so deeply. Some women say it makes them feel less valuable, and no one deserves to feel like that. Also, it is very difficult, maybe impossible, to re-gain the trust you spent months or years earning. All of that can be lost in 5 minutes. The damage done to your word and your reputation can be permanent. Relationship commitments are a contract that **you sign with your word**. When you break that contract you lose some of the power of your word. When you say anything after that, people are less likely to believe you. And that mistrust can spill over into other areas of your life: *"If he couldn't honor a simple agreement he made with his girlfriend then maybe I can't trust him to work with me at a job…"*

Using women

Men use women for lots of things. Some men collect women like stamps, baseball cards, shells on a beach or whatever young people collect these days (hmm, I'm really not sure what young people collect anymore… I'm getting distracted. *This part must be hard for me*). It seems like men just collect women for fun, but there's usually more to it. Some men are trying to 'look cool'. Some believe in polygamy. Some may have a sexual addiction. A lot of men are just copying what they see entertainers, athletes and other men do.

When I collected women, it was more about their interest in me. I was using women for attention. I don't drink or smoke so I had to figure out something else to do when I got sad. Instead, I would spend time with a woman who I knew liked me. That usually made me feel better. I later realized it was more about insecurity. There were areas in my own life that I wasn't satisfied with. There were things about myself that I didn't like. I didn't feel whole or complete on my own. So I used women to fill in those gaps. As long as I had women around who admired me, I didn't have to think as much about the ways I didn't love my own self.

There were a couple of problems with that. One was that after a woman gave me her attention and I felt better again, I didn't need her anymore. That created lots of mess, because then I'd have all these unwanted obligations to women at my school or job, etc. The other even worse problem was that I never learned to enjoy being alone. I never really got to know myself or learn to love my own company. And you can't really begin to form a healthy relationship with anyone else until you do that with yourself.

This is from a blog I wrote on MySpace in 2008:

"I've hurt every woman I've ever been with. Some really bad. I've also become really good at creating drama in my life to distract

me from having to live with myself. That's part of my journey, and it's unfair that other people have had to suffer because of it. Me and The Lady were having one of our last conversations in our apartment tonight and I had an epiphany in the middle of a conversation about things that weren't the point. That's why I'm writing this. It feels appropriate to share it as publicly as she has shared her love for me. Interestingly, my epiphany came in the form of advice to her. I'm not sure where it came from, but it kept repeating over and over in my head as I lay there hiding tears while she solemnly packed her belongings. The voice said to her, through me: 'Love, whatever you do, never again give too much of yourself in a relationship with a man who doesn't love or like himself. He will, always, eventually leave you or push you away, if only to protect you from himself.'"

<u>Ignoring my gut</u>

This mistake has caused me more trouble than all of them put together. In many ways it is a combination of them. Before I've lied or cheated or used women there's always something inside of me telling me not to do it. But I ignored it, or wasn't paying close enough attention to hear it.

"Ignoring your gut" means not listening to that inner voice that guides us all through life. It's like your conscience, or your intuition. It's the voice that comes from inside the depths of your soul, the place where your wisdom lives. You could also think about it as a voice that comes from the outside, if you believe in guardian angels, orishas, or your ancestors watching over you and guiding your steps. Wherever it comes from, it's always there. And when I'm quiet, tuned it, paying attention, I can hear it and it helps me make the right decisions. Ignoring that voice has resulted in some disasters for me.

So there was this girl… (Some of the best and the worst stories start off like that.) She was beautiful, smart, and very talented. I met her when I was 23 or 24. We had a lot in common and were attracted to each other. We decided pretty quickly to commit. It was an intense relationship. We moved fast. I had clothes in her apartment. We traveled to different cities to visit both our families. The possibility of the 'M' word came up in our conversations. We were on a long-term path, even though it lasted less than a year.

We fought a lot. I can't even remember why. We fought more than I've fought with any other person before or after. That should've been enough reason to walk away but I stayed, even though many days it felt like a really bad idea. I also stayed because our good times were just as wonderful as our bad times were ugly. Until it eventually became too much and we broke up. That should've been a simple end to a typical relationship story, but not for me. Not when I'm ignoring my gut.

A week after we broke up my father drowned. He was on a small boat with his friend that flipped over in a lake. The friend swam back but my dad didn't. It's a suspicious story because my dad had been a lifeguard, traveled the world scuba diving, and was an expert swimmer. I've watched him swim for miles in the ocean and come back ready for more. But all we got back on that tragic October day was a body and a story. I eventually made peace knowing I might not ever know what really happened that day, but at the time I was in shock.

I was away at school when Dad died. It had only been a week since I broke up with my ex, but I was already pursuing another lady. I was in the apartment of the new girl when I got the phone call about Dad. My older brother told me the news and I immediately wanted to drive home, but my car was too old to make the trip. Among my options for potential cars to borrow that night was my ex-girlfriend's car. She convinced me to fly home in the morning instead of driving 11 hours in the dark crying. I slept in my ex's apartment that night. Her desire to ease my pain and my need to be comforted led to us having sex. Later, my ex started telling people I raped her that night.

A lot of what happened during the months after Dad is a blur. There was a beautiful funeral, lots of phone calls, I think people brought food to the house. I went back to school. It was November of 2005 so the semester was ending soon. I can't really remember what it felt like. My ex was very supportive during my grieving. It felt like being re-introduced to a sweet side of her that I forgot existed. She was so sweet that I thought breaking up had been a mistake. But there was still also the new girl, who was also very sweet and supportive. I was confused about which way to go: the old familiar ex or the excitement of a new girl. I didn't know which to choose, so I didn't. I picked them both, and lied to them both about each other.

What I really needed at the time was to choose myself and allow myself time to grieve, but I wasn't that smart yet. I spent months trying to develop a new relationship with a new woman while still spending time with my ex. I was telling both of them on the nights that I wasn't with them that I was going to my own apartment. It was a total mess. I was insisting to both of them that I was just friends with the other. I eventually got caught. The ex saw me holding hands with the new girl at grocery store. That was the last time I ever spoke to the ex.

The next day my ex wrote a blog that she called her 'resignation letter' and that was the end of us. Soon after I was asked to teach drumming to children at a school but one of the parents heard the rumor my ex was spreading about me raping her. So a council of elders was organized to deal with it. It was the most embarrassing process I've ever been through. My personal life and my character were dissected like a science experiment in a room full of community leaders whom I admired. They met with me and my ex several times to hear our sides of the story. I was required to have a spiritual reading done. I did everything they asked me to because I didn't have anything to hide. At the conclusion, they decided that my ex and I should never speak to each other again. If we're ever in the same room we should each pretend like the other doesn't exist, and we've been doing that since 2005.

I eventually went to the school to teach drumming and moved on with my life. I built a beautiful relationship with the "new girl" that lasted a couple of years and a friendship with her that I hope lasts a lifetime. But an accusation like rape is one of the worst rumors that can be attached to a man's name. Just knowing there were people in the world who might've thought about me as a rapist sent me into a deep depression. I have been fortunate in the years after to not have any disruptions or any opportunities blocked because of the accusation. My reputation, character and support systems have protected me. But that situation forever changed the way I interact with women during intimate moments.

Men should never have sex without obvious **consent**. We should never do anything without knowing 100% that she wants to do it. That was the mistake I made with my ex. She never said "No" or "Stop" but she may have had doubt in her mind at the time. Our relationship was already too messy to complicate it further with sex. I've been extremely careful ever since to not be intimate with a woman who was even a little <u>unsure</u>.

Oftentimes, the man feels responsible for initiating the sexual activity. It seems to be the man's job to make the advances and the woman either accepts or rejects them. A lot of women would not want to appear too forward sexually because of the double standard -- we proudly call men pimps if they have a lot of sex, but we call women whores if they also like sex a lot. So what happens in the bedroom is the man feels like he has to keep pushing even after a little resistance. That's when you hear a guy saying *"Come on baby. It'll be okay, just relax. I know you want to, please just a little..."* Or worse, guys will use their strength to try to control her movement. If you ever find yourself in that position, **stop immediately**.

It's never worth getting sex or affection from a woman if she doesn't completely want to give it. Even if you can be persistent and eventually wear her down by begging and making promises. You just don't want it like that. Because even if she kinda gives you consent in the moment, she might think back on it later and feel like you took advantage of her. Especially if drugs, alcohol or confusing emotions are involved. I've learned that the best physical intimacy happens when you know with such certainty that the woman wants to do it that she is almost begging you. Not the other way around. Consent is sexy.

Re-Pairing Cycles

We all come from our parents. Every human is still a result of one man combined with one woman; technology has not outsmarted that design yet. So there must be something valuable still to learn from parents. We can't avoid their impact on who we become. Even if your mother or father wasn't active in your life, you are still affected by their absence. Their DNA still swims through your blood and shows up in your personality even if you never met them.

Our parents are often our first example of how a relationship looks. We learn how to be in relationships from watching them, whether we think we're paying attention or not. They don't have to be your biological parents. Whatever adult relationships you saw while you were growing up were your first teacher. Sometimes the relationships we see from our parents and other adults are good, and sometimes they are bad. More often, they are mixed.

I started writing this book after my parents were gone. There's so much I wish I could've asked them: about how they met, what they liked about each other, how they learned to communicate, what they appreciated and regretted most about their relationship. I know they both felt like they made mistakes during their marriage. And I'm sure they wouldn't want their children to repeat their mistakes. That's why this section is important. Each generation has the responsibility of stopping the negative cycles that we inherit from our parents and grandparents. To REPAIR our communities by bringing strong healthy partnerships back into our families.

I didn't get to talk directly to my parents about their relationship, but I've been able to learn a lot about their marriage through their letters, journals, and cards left around the house (lucky for me, they didn't have the internet yet). I found stuff that was really hard to read and information that I was never supposed to see. The most useful part of this process was being able to examine the writings of my parents and compare them with my own exchanges with women in my life.

My Parents Letters

My parents had a difficult relationship from the very beginning; there were always doubts. My mother wrote this to my father when she was 20 years old, before they got married: *"I know you say you love me but why and do you really think you want to be with me for the rest of your life? Right now when I think of being married to you I don't feel as if I will be happy because I'll always be competing for your love. Everytime I'm around you I'm reminded of this and I just feel that I should get out of your life before it's too late… But Thabiti I love you too much to do that."*

Thankfully they worked it out, got married, had four incredible children (*pats self on back*), and created a household that I remember being full of love! Here's a note my father wrote in 1991 to my 35-year-old mother:

"I finally succomed & am here writing down some of my thoughts as a "special" birthday present. We both know how rare it is for me to document, "written-wise", how I feel, think, communicate, express & otherwise show my expression of appreciation for having you in my life. For the record, so to speak, I have been loving you since the 1st day on 64th Beach that I laid eyes on you & that's been some 15–16 years ago…We've been through just about every scenario imaginable thru our years together, with most being positive & favorable. You truly are a wonderful, thoughtful, kind, sincere, patient, loving, genuine, intelligent, woman." [Aug.16, 1991]

But their happy times didn't seem to last long. A couple of years later Ma was writing this to Dad:

"Another restless night. I don't know if it's more important to try to maintain family peace or try to find inner peace. I don't seem to be able to achieve both in this situation. The thoughts of what you may be involved in at any particular moment during your nights away wakes me almost every hour. I don't know how people stay

together or break apart in these situations. Do you?? Would you tolerate this discomfort? Help!!! –CJ" [12-19-1995]

Their issue was a pretty straightforward one. Dad believed in a different type of family structure than Mom. Dad wanted to have relationships and children with multiple women and Mom married one guy expecting it to stay that way. Dad wasn't clear enough about what he wanted when they first got married. Here's a note from Dad to Ma:

"Like I said yesterday if I had only been mature enough in the early days of our relationship bonding to express my true inner thoughts probably all of this pain and confusion could have been avoided. The only thing wrong with that scenario is #1 our love would not have grown to the level that it is and our darling children wouldn't have been on the planet in the form that they are."

"I know it sounds like "my cake and eat it too" b.s. but I truly feel that the lifestyle I ascribe to has real merit in these times though it seems to you unbearable at times. It really aint no ego trip or no sexual fantasy type relationships that's being established but more based on commitment, concern and children." [10-23-1995]

However, in the middle of their marriage and trying to work out a structure that made sense for everybody, my father was having relationships that produced more children. This is Ma's thoughts about it written in her journal:

I have been interacting more with Thabiti daughters. I keep trying to see them outside of vivid images of Thabiti and another woman creation but they favor their respective mothers so much that I haven't been able too....I don't mind interacting with them. I just wish he knew how it felt so that he could be more courteous, complementary and sensitive to what I am going through. Once I heard today that he and Obari went to *****'s I was very upset and thought that he should of known not to take any of my children to their houses right now." [Sept. 17, 1996]

From the mid 90s on, it seemed like my parents' marriage was just getting worse and worse. In 1994 Ma wrote, *"The pain is increasing instead of decreasing with time. It is deeply internal, seeming eternal. It has taken over my being my every-other thought and movement is a reflection of it."* I found a page that Ma typed out in April of 1994 with the heading "CERTIFICATE OF DEATH" that inspired the title of this book. Mom wrote about Dad's symbolic death: *"May his soul be extended to all those lonely women out there who have been secretly receiving his loving and intimacy during his said marriage. May they now abide in the place that they have so patiently and sneakily waited for in the rebirth of Thabiti Cartman the Ladies Man."*

Dad also offered the occasional apology:

"Dear Carla,

I Thabiti apologize in the deepest sense for all that I have done to you. I know that my deeds have touched every sense of your being. Your dedicated love to a man that you thought was honest and dedicated to a monogamous relationship for our sixteen years together has been shaken to the roots by the deception I created."

But it wasn't enough. Mom became depressed. She sacrificed her happiness to stay home for her children. I'm sure they would've gotten divorced as soon as my youngest brother went to college, if Dad hadn't died before that.

Then, after his death, Mom suddenly became in charge of managing the property Dad owned. She had to deal with the grief and confusion of his drowning. The other women joined together and took Mom to court for access to money for their children, and it all seems to have been too overwhelming. For a long time the doctors didn't have an explanation for it. The psychiatrist sent me to a neurologist who sent me back to the psychiatrist. But we all knew what happened. Mom decided to go on a mental vacation. She wrote about it before she left:

Dear Family,

I'm sorry that I can't handle the pains of the world. But I really can't. It's nobodies fault but mine. My mind and heart were just not built to handle this kind of pain…
You are strong, beautiful, wonderful and loving children. Have happy wonderful lives and don't wallow in my grief. Know that I am in a better and more peaceful place. I can feel no more pain. No more pain!

My Letters

I learned a lot about myself reading my parents' letters and then comparing them to conversations I've had with women. I remember being a teenager and vowing to never be like my dad. I hated the way he made my mother feel. I promised myself that I would never make a woman feel that way. Then I got to college and received a letter in 2001 from my girlfriend after she caught me cheating:

"Hearing what happened and knowing that it was real, shut my body down. Never in my life has someone made me feel numb inside as if my heart stopped... I was fully aware of your past so I was prepared for the worse, as time went on and your reassured me that you had too much to lose by making mistakes like this and it was easier than you thought it would be to stay faithful, I let my guard down. Something I will think 100x more before I let it happen again... I can't be with someone who could disrespect me the way you did. Who did you think you were by holding onto my heart while you weighed your options. I think that was really selfish of you."

Eventually, I learned to make the difficult decision to leave a relationship before bringing other women into it. This is from an email I wrote in 2007:

"The man in me that is trying to learn to make decisions and not just let them be made on my behalf told me that there is another option than selfishness and deceipt. it's a little harder. it might hurt her temporarily. its going to make you really sad to lose her. people are going to be mad at you. your rent's going to double and you'll be sleeping on the floor. it's much less convenient. it's unlike what you're used to doing, etc. AND it's the responsible thing to do right now. she deserves better. and it's time for you to man up."

Dating and flirting with a lot of women has brought consistent problems into my relationships. I was always having trust issues and women said they often didn't feel like they were enough for me. That's part of the baggage that comes with a "ladies man" reputation. It's a credibility problem. Often, when I'm with a woman who I'm genuinely interested in, she has a hard time believing me. My girlfriend explains it well in an email from 2009:

"I never fully allowed myself to be all that I can be in a relationship with you for fear of being hurt. I want to cook for you. But I am afraid of it not being good enough. I want to sing to you. But I am afraid another woman can do it better. I would love to dance freely WITH you, write pieces together and be naked. And yet you will always know better dancers, more talented writers and seen fatter assess…..There are times when I forget that there are other women running the race along side me. In those times, I am so enraptured with our synergy that those other presence seem like blurs in the background."

Revisiting these old emails and letters reminds me that this becoming a man thing is an ongoing process. It's not a place you get to where you can finally say "Yes! I made it." I'm 34 now and have matured a lot, but still have a ways to go. No matter how old you get there's always gonna be stuff to work on, to improve about yourself. And that's not bad news. It's exciting when you commit to the adventure of being human. Anything that stops learning and growing, is dead.

My Most Important Relationship

I've been in a bunch of different types of relationships: dating, long term, cohabiting, friendships, friendships with benefits. I've liked, loved, been in love, hated, broken hearts, had my heart broken. But none of those relationships have been as intense and rich and fulfilling as the one I'm in right now, with my son. He's two and half years old, and he's the best thing that ever happened to me. Fatherhood is a so beautiful. I pray that I can be as good a father to him as my dad was to me. I'll never understand why so many men choose to miss out on such incredible relationships with their children. I do understand, though, that it's difficult to have a good relationship with your kids if you don't have a good relationship with their mother.

I'm not married to my child's mother. We dated for a little while and were soon blessed with a sweet surprise. Well, not exactly sweet at first. First it was scary. We didn't think we were ready. Our relationship was having ups and downs. I couldn't afford no baby. But we worked it out. Which didn't have to mean staying in a romantic relationship. Marriage can be a beautiful thing when it's done right, but just because you have a kid together doesn't always mean you would be the best romantic partners for each other.

For me, having a baby together was more of a commitment than getting married would've been. We'll be co-parents for life. So we're still in a relationship. My son's well-being partially depends on the health of my relationship with his mother. We still have to work on communication, and sharing, and sacrifice, and trust, and honesty, and even love. All the stuff we would've had to maintain if we were together romantically. And it's still work sometimes, but worth it because my son is worth it.

Conclusion

I appreciate you letting me share my life and my thoughts with you. Just by reading this you have already begun to defy the stereotypes that say young Black men don't care about nothing, don't read, and can't think for themselves. I challenge you now to share this book with some of your friends. Spend some time talking about what you like and don't like about it, where you agree and disagree. And remember this is just the beginning of the conversation. There's lots more books to read. You'll never hear anyone say they regret reading too much.

There's more to being a good man than I mention in this book. A lot of it you'll have to discover on your own. And from other men and women you respect, and from documentaries, and good conversations, and just from sitting still in silence. That's the work we must all do. Myself included. To seek excellence. To be disciplined. To love each other. To stop procrastinating and making excuses. To not settle. To keep family first. To eat better, grow our own food when we can. To exercise our minds and our bodies. To follow our passions. To take care of our own. And to dream and work beyond our comfort zones. Until all people are free.

BIBLIOGRAPHY

Akbar, Na'im. *Visions for Black Men.* Tallahassee, FL: Mind Productions & Associates, 1991.

Akbar, Na'im. *Breaking the Chains of Psychological Slavery.* Tallahassee, FL: Mind Productions and Associates, 1996.

Akbar, Na'im. *Know Thy Self.* Tallahassee, FL: Mind Productions and Associates, 1998.

Belton, Don (editor). *Speak My Name: Black Men on Masculinity and the American Dream.* Boston: Beacon Press, 1995.

Billingsley, Andrew. *Black Families in White America.* New York: Simon and Schuster, 1968.

Breitman, George (edited with prefatory notes). *Malcolm X Speaks: Selected Speeches and Statements.* New York, Merit Publishers, 1965.

Connor, Marlene Kim. *What is Cool? Understanding Black Manhood in America.* Chicago: Agate, 1995.

Davidson, Basil. *The African Slave Trade (A Revised and Expanded Edition).* Boston: little, brown and company, 1961.

Frazier, E. Franklin. *The Negro Family in the United States (Revised and Abridged).* Chicago: The University of Chicago Press, 1939.

Franklin, Anderson. *From Brotherhood to Manhood: How Black Men Rescue Their Relationships and Dreams from the Invisibility Syndrome.* Wiley and Sons, 2004.

Fu-Kiau, Kimbwandende Kia Bunseki. *Self-Healing Power and Therapy: Old Teachings from Africa.* Baltimore, Imprint Editions, 1991.

Gilroy, Paul. *The Black Atlantic: Modernity and Double Consciousness*. Cambridge, Mass: Harvard University Press, 1993.

Gutman, Herbert G. *The Black Family in Slavery and Freedom 1750-1925*. Random House, 1976.

Hendrix, Harville. *Getting the Love You Want: A Guide for Couples*. Harper Perennial, 1988.

Hilliard, Asa G. T*he Maroon Within Us: Selected Essays on African American Community Socialization*. Baltimore, MD: Black Classic Press, 1995.

Hilliard, Asa G. *SBA: The Reawakening of the African Mind*. Gainesville, FL: Makare Publishing: 1997.

hooks, bell. *Killing Rage: Ending Racism*. New York: Henry Holt and Company, 1995.

hooks, bell. *Salvation: Black People and Love*. Perennial, 2001.

hooks, bell. *The Will to Change: Men, Masculinity and Love*. New York: Atria Books, 2004.

Hutchinson, Earl Ofari. *The Assassination of the Black Male Image*. New York: Simon & Schuster Paperbacks, 1994.

Johnson, Ernest H. *Brothers on the Mend: Understanding and Healing Anger for African-American Men and Women*. New York: Pocket Books, 1998.

Kunjufu, Jawanza. *State of Emergency: We Must Save African American Males*. Chicago, IL: African-American Images, 2001.

Lindsay, Lisa A. *Captives as Commodities: The Transatlantic Slave Trade*. New Jersey: Prentice Hall, 2008.

Madhubuti, Haki R. *Black Men: Obsolete, Singe, Dangerous? The Afrikan American Family in Transition*. Chicago: Third World Press, 1991.

Madhubuti, Haki R. *Tough Notes: A Healing Call for Creating Exceptional Black Men*. Chicago: Third World Press, 2002.

Neal, Mark Anthony. *New Black Man*. New York: Routledge, 2006.

Perry, Steve. *Man Up! Nobody is Coming to Save Us*. Middletown, CT: Renegade, 2005.

Smith, Mark M.(editor). *Stono: Documenting and Interpreting a Southern Slave Revolt*. University of South Carolina Press, 2005.

Vanzant, Iyanla. *The Spirit of a Man: A Vision of Transformation for Black Men and the Women Who Love Them*. San Francisco: HarperCollins Publishers, 1996.

Williams, Chancelor. *The Destruction of Black Civilization: Great Issues of a Race from 4500 B.C. to 2000 A.D.* Chicago, IL: Third World Press, 1974.

Wilson, Amos N. *The Falsification of Afrikan Consciousness: Eurocentric History, Psychiatry and the Politics of White Supremacy*. New York: Afrikan World InfoSystems, 1993.

Wilson, Amos N. *Understanding Black Adolescent Male Violence: It's Remediation and Prevention*. New York: Afrikan World Systems, 1992.

NOTES

Chapter 1

1. Smith, M.D. (2014, February 14). White People Have to Give Up Racism. http://www.thenation.com/blog/, date accessed: March 26, 2014.

2. Jacobson, Matthew Frye, Whiteness of a Different Color: European Immigrants and the Alchemy of Race (Cambridge, Massachusetts: Harvard University Press, 1998), p.1.

3. Luhby, Tami. (2012, June 21). Worsening Wealth Inequality by Race. http://money.cnn.com/2012/06/21/news/economy/wealth-gap-race/, date accessed: May 5, 2013.

4. Dyer, Ervin. (2007, March 31). Invisible Men: Many Young Black Males Are in Crisis. http://www.post-gazette.com/invisible-men/2007/05/31/Invisible-Men-Many-young-black-males-are-in-crisis/stories, date accessed: May 5, 2013

5. Pittsburg's Racial Demographics 2015: Differences and Disparities. University of Pittsburg School of Social Work; Center on Race and Social Problems. http://www.crsp.pitt.edu/sites/default/files/Final%20version%20for%20publishing.pdf, date accessed March 4, 2015.

6. See Pittsburg's Racial Demographics 2015: Differences and Disparities.

7. Holland, Jesse J. (2014, April 3). National Urban League State of Black America 2014 Report Says Minorities Losign Economic Ground. http://www.huffingtonpost.com/2014/04/03/national-urban-league-state-of-black-america_n_5083025.html, date accessed March 5, 2015.

8. Laverde-Hansen, Lyonel. (2015, February 25). Black Men in U.S. Prisons Could Fill the Prisons of Eight Countries Combined. http://yourblackworld.net/2015/02/25/black-

men-in-u-s-prisons-could-fill-the-prisons-of-8-countries-combined/, date accessed March 5, 2015.

9. The Silent Genocide: Facts about the Devastating Plight of Black Males in America. (2014, June 4). Black Star Journal.http://blackstarjournal.org/?p=4142, date accessed, March 5, 2015.

10. Rennison, C.M & Welchans, S. (2000, July 14). Intimate Partner Violence- A report by the Bureau of Justice Statistics.http://www.ojp.usdoj.gov/bjs/pub/ascii/ipv.txt, date accessed: August 12, 2013

11. American Bar Association-Commission Domestic and Sexual Violence. http://www.americanbar.org/groups/domestic_violence/resources/statistics.html, date accessed: August 12, 2013

12. Hart & Rennison, 2003. Bureau of Justice Statistics Special Report, U.S. Department of Justice.http://www.wcsap.org/african-american-community, date accessed: March 5, 2015.

13. (2015, February 25). How the Myth of the Strong Black Women Hurts Rape Victims. North Dallas Gazette.http://northdallasgazette.com/2015/02/25/how-the-myth-of-the-strong-black-women-hurts-rape-victims/, date accessed March 5, 2015.

14. See American Bar Association

Chapter 2

1. Morton, Janks & Toldson, Ivory A. Black People Don't Read. (iYAGO Entertainment Group, 2012).

2. Lindsey, Lisa A. Captives as Commodities: The Transatlantic Slave Trade. (New Jersey: Pearson Prentice Hall, 2008).

3. Davidson, Basil. The African Slave Trade [A revised and expanded edition]. (Boston: Little, brown and company, 1980), p.113.

4. See Lindsey (2008)

5. Williams, Brian. (2000, March 13). Grave Site Exposes Brutality of Slavery in Early New York. The Militant, Vol 64 (10). http://www.themilitant.com/2000/6410/641060.html

6. Lopresti, Rob. Which U.S. Presidents Owned Slaves. http://home.nas.com/lopresti/ps.htm, date accessed: August 22, 2013

7. Jackson, Vanessa. In Our Own Voices: African American Stories of Oppression, Survival and Recovery in the Mental Health System…

8. Billingsly, Andrew. Black Families in White America. (New York: Simon and Schuster, 1968)

9. See Billingsly (1968)

10. See Billingsly (1968), p.60

11. See Billingsly (1968), p.60

12. See Morton and Toldson (2012)

13. http://www.naacp.org/blog/entry/know-your-worth-if-we-dont-know-we-cant-grow-our-community

14. Film: "The Life and Times of Sarah Baartman" directed by Zola Maseko

Chapter 4

1. Bynum, Edward Bruce (editor). Why Darkness Matters: The Power of Melanin in the Brain. African American Images, 2005.

2. West, Kanye. From song "Power" on My Beautiful Dark Twisted Fantasy album. Roc-a Fella Records, 2010.

3. This section is adapted from a model I learned called "Feelings as Messengers" from Wekesa and Afiya Madzimiyo of AyaEd.com

4. Hendrix, Harville. Getting the Love You Want Workbook:

The New Couples' Study Guide. Atria Books; 1 edition, 2003.

5. Powell, Kevin. The Vibe Q: Tupac Shakur, Ready to Live. (Vibe, April 11, 1995) p 52.

6. Wilson, Amos. Blueprint for Black Power: A Moral, Political, and Economic Imperative for the Twenty-First Century. Afrikan World Infosystems, 1998.

7. Hilliard, David & Weise, Donald (editors). The Huey P. Newton Reader. New York: Seven Stories Press, 2002.

8. From a Bernard Kinsey lecture I attended at the National Black Educators Association conference, October 13th, 2012

STUDY GUIDE FOR POSITIVE MALE DEVELOPMENT
OR
THE STUFF THAT HELPED ME ON MY MANHOOD JOURNEY

1. Book: Visions for Black Men by Na'im Akbar

2. Book: The Falsification of Afrikan Consciousness by Amos Wilson

3. Documentary: Hip Hop- Beyond Beats and Rhymes by Byron Hurt

4. The Spirit of a Man: A Vision of Transformation for Black Men and the Women Who Love Them by Iyanla Vanzant

5. Song: Thieves in the Nights by Black Star

6. Book: Parable of the Sower by Octavia E. Butler

7. Film: Bamboozled by Spike Lee

8. Book: Killing Rage by bell hooks

9. Book: The Reawakening of the African Mind by Asa G. Hilliard, III

10. Album: Let's Get Free by Dead Prez

11. Book and Film: The Spook Who Sat by the Door by Sam Greenlee

12. Book: Malcolm X Speaks edited by George Breitman

13. Book: The Healers by Ayi Kwei Armah

14. Song: Shuffering and Shmiling by Fela Kuti

15. Book: Self Healing Power and Therapy by Kimbwandende Kia Bunseki Fu-Kiau

16. Book: The Prisoner's Wife: A Memoir by Asha Bandele

17. Book: Intellectual Warfare by Jacob H. Carruthers

18. Documentary: A great and Mighty Walk by John Henrik Clark

19. Book: Black Men: Obsolete, Singe, Dangerous? The Afrikan American Family in Transition by Haki Madhubuti

20. Books: Countering the Conspiracy to Destroy Black Boys by Jawanza Kunjufu

SYMBOLS

Chapter 1

Gola Glyph: Hepicat/Hipi

"One who stays woke."

"This Soul, Body, Mind is woke to the world."

Hepicat represents a conscious, active individual or community. In this sense, consciousness is an awareness of the individual/ communities reality. This person is woke to their political/cultural/ economic conditions but not broken by them.

Hepicat is an aware state of mind, that is not easily overwhelmed or broken.

Hepicat is a sharp state of mind, that brings a calm, levelheaded approach when taking action.

Hepicat is the Warrior's mentality.

Chapter 2

Gola Glyph: Blues

"Tragedy don't come in vain/ It comes so we might be courageous/ to fulfill our obligation to our God and all creation /and stand in determination/able to look death in the face/and say we made it/ we made it/ we made it." -adapted from "We Made It" by Sunni Patterson

Blues is Our ability to take what we know about surviving hatred, going to sleep with anger, of hitting rock-bottom, and of experiencing a walk on Cloud 9 and then transform our pain and joy into something magnificent--something that keeps us fighting through the pain. The Glyph shows a Ship inside of a Guitar: the glyph represents the ways we survive Enslavement and Oppression in America by remixing our pain into the medicine we need to keep alive.

Chapter 3

Gola Glyph: Griot/Jeg-na/Jali

The symbol has two interpretations:

1. This is a teacher dressed in the robes and mask of a mystic
2. This is the house of an oracle/teacher/guide projecting light from the top of a mountain.

Griot symbolizes someone who leads you into a period of transformation and self-actualization. Griot represents the master educator, not the expert—so people who have mastered the act of teaching/mentoring/transferring knowledge.

Chapter 4

Akoben
-Inspired by the Akan of Ghana and the Afrikans of New Orleans.

"Dare to Struggle, Dare to Win.
If you don't dare to struggle, then God-Damnit you don't deserve to win!
Let me say peace to you if you're willing to fight for it."

-Chairman Fred Hampton, the Chicago Black Panthers

Akoben in the Akan culture is a War Horn, when people hear it's call they know its time to get ready for battle. It is no different here. The Gola Glyph of Akoben is a trumpet spitting revolutionary fire, and everyone who catches the fire best be ready for action. We sound Akoben here in Black America and the Diaspora to let everyone know that Now is the time to Struggle, to fight, to get free.

Chapter 5

Gola Glyph: 'Huru - "My presence Liberates."

Huru is The Big Heart, your Soul at its most vulnerable, raw, creative, and generous state—thus, free and liberated. Huru represents our transformation into culture warriors, the people protect our communities, provide for our people when no one else will or can, and help create community uplift.

Huru represents the union between the liberating presence and creative mind.

Dane Verrtah is a Black cultural artist, community engaged educator, designer and researcher-activist from New Orleans, LA. His passion and work centers on creating bridges between communities and youth in the African continent and the Americas. He is a Master's degree candidate at the University of Minnesota Twin Cities where he researches methods for creating Afrikan-Centered Education Systems and the impacts of Afrocentric Education on Black youth. Brother Verrtah comes from a family of artists and educators in one of the African Diaspora's most unique and creative cities; at an early age he witnessed the power of art to embolden, heal, and transform people surviving oppression. Using an action-based, interdisciplinary approach to research, he seeks to creatively disrupt and dismantle systems of oppression throughout the global Black community.

Through his GOLA Language Project/Hepicat, he hopes to create a symbol-based language that tells the stories of Black people in the Americas. He dreams and struggles for the day when his people will no longer see themselves as a race, but as a Nation and Culture.

For more on Hepicat:

www.hepicat.us

wehepicat.tumblr.com

facebook.com/WeHepicat

120916-500-1-60W(Sept2016)